W9-BGP-240

RL
9.8
Pt.
5

The Music
Library

The History of
Rap & Hip-Hop

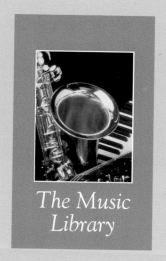

The Music
Library

The History of
Rap & Hip-Hop

By Soren Baker

LUCENT BOOKS
An imprint of Thomson Gale, a part of The Thomson Corporation

THOMSON
★
GALE

™

Detroit • New York • San Francisco • San Diego • New Haven, Conn. • Waterville, Maine • London • Munich

GUMDROP BOOKS
PO44118
SPRING 08
$ 25.95

LIBRARY OF CONGRESS CATALOGING-IN-PUBLICATION DATA

Baker, Soren, 1975–
   The history of rap and hip-hop / by Soren Baker.
      p. cm. — (The music library)
Includes bibliographical references (p.) and index.
ISBN 1-59018-739-3 (hard cover : alk. paper)
1. Rap (Music)—History and criticism—Juvenile literature. 2. Hip-hop—Juvenile literature. I. Title. II. Series: Music library (San Diego, Calif.)
ML3531.B35 2006
782.421649'09—dc22

2005015542

Printed in the United States of America

• Contents •

• Foreword •

In the nineteenth century, English novelist Charles Kingsley wrote, "Music speaks straight to our hearts and spirits, to the very core and root of our souls. . . . Music soothes us, stirs us up . . . melts us to tears." As Kingsley stated, music is much more than just a pleasant arrangement of sounds. It is the resonance of emotion, a joyful noise, a human endeavor that can soothe the spirit or excite the soul. Musicians can also imitate the expressive palate of the earth, from the violent fury of a hurricane to the gentle flow of a babbling brook.

The word *music* is derived from the fabled Greek muses, the children of Apollo who ruled the realms of inspiration and imagination. Composers have long called upon the muses for help and insight. Music is not merely the result of emotions and pleasurable sensations, however.

Music is a discipline subject to formal study and analysis. It involves the juxtaposition of creative elements such as rhythm, melody, and harmony with intellectual aspects of composition, theory, and instrumentation. Like painters mixing red, blue, and yellow into thousands of colors, musicians blend these various elements to create classical symphonies, jazz improvisations, country ballads, and rock-and-roll tunes.

Throughout centuries of musical history, individual musical elements have been blended and modified in infinite ways. The resulting sounds may convey a whole range of moods, emotions, reactions, and messages. Music, then, is both an expression and reflection of human experience and emotion.

The foundations of modern musical styles were laid down by the first ancient musicians who used wood, rocks, animal skins—and their own bodies—to re-create the sounds of the natural world in which they lived. With their hands, their feet, and their very breath they ignited the passions of listeners and moved them to their feet. The dancing, in turn, had a mesmerizing and hypnotic effect that allowed people to transcend their worldly concerns. Through music they could achieve a level of shared experience that could not be found in other forms of communication. For this reason, music has always been part of religious endeavors, from ancient Egyptian religious ceremonies to modern Christian masses. And it has inspired dance movements from kings and queens spinning the minuet to punk rockers slamming together in a mosh pit.

By examining musical genres ranging from Western classical music to rock and roll, readers will find a new understanding of old music and develop an appreciation for new sounds. Books in Lucent's Music Library focus on the music, the musicians, the instruments, and on music's place in cultural history. The songs and artists examined may be easily found in the CD and sheet music collections of local libraries so that readers may study and enjoy the music covered in the books. Informative sidebars, annotated bibliographies, and complete indexes highlight the text in each volume and provide young readers with many opportunities for further discussion and research.

Hip-Hop Culture

In the past thirty years, hip-hop culture has grown from its humble beginnings in the South Bronx section of New York City into a significant and influential cultural movement. Created in the mid-1970s by poor Bronx residents with few resources, hip-hop has become a billion-dollar industry whose reach now stretches around the world. Hip-hop has influenced the way people make music, the way they dance, and the way they wear their clothes. It has also shaped people's political views and turned many people into entrepreneurs.

Hip-hop culture encompasses four main components: rapping, DJing, graffiti art, and B-boying (break dancing). At its inception, hip-hop was inspired by a variety of other art forms, many of which still influence and inspire hip-hop artists today. One of hip-hop's key characteristics is its ability to take an idea, a practice, or a way of doing something and make it into something new. For instance, spoken-word

poets such as The Last Poets, Gil Scott-Heron, and Rudy Ray Moore, artists who recited rhyming lyrics over a musical backing, inspired rappers. Early hip-hop DJs invented a new way to enjoy music by repeating song passages best suited for dancing, while graffiti artists went from writing their names on buildings and billboards to creating dazzling art showcased in galleries. B-boys, also known as boogie boys or break-dancers, created a new style of dance featuring acrobatic skills.

Rap Takes Control

The most popular component of hip-hop culture is rap. Even though the words *hip-hop* and *rap* are often used interchangeably, they are not the same thing. Rap is part of a larger culture, while hip-hop is the culture itself. When people refer to hip-hop music, they typically mean rap, even though hip-hop music also includes other musical genres, such as rhythm & blues

(R&B), soul, funk, jazz, and even rock and roll.

The first major rap recording was "Rapper's Delight," released in 1979 by the Sugarhill Gang. By the mid-1980s, rap music was the dominant part of hip-hop culture. In early rap recordings, rappers typically performed over music made by musicians who simply copied the original music of other artists. By the mid-1980s, however, sampling and advances in technology and studio equipment (most significantly drum machines) changed the way rap was made. Sampling allowed producers, the people in rap who make the music, to incorporate segments of the original recordings of other artists into the producers' own material. Today, rap is made in a number of ways, including sampling and playing live music.

The way in which people rap has also evolved. Rappers in the 1970s favored a simple, straightforward style. The lyrics of most early rap songs focused on having a good time and boasted about the ability of a DJ or the lyrical prowess of the rapper. By the mid-1980s, known as the golden era of rap, rappers had developed complex deliveries and a number of rhyme styles to complement the explosion in sounds and kinds of music

A B-boy performs on the sidewalk. B-boying, also known as break dancing, is a major component of hip-hop culture.

Popular hip-hop artist Kanye West performs for enthusiastic fans at the Los Angeles Coliseum in 2005. Hip-hop music has gained a large following since the 1970s.

being produced. Today, rappers make songs about virtually everything. For instance, 50 Cent favors a gangster style that reflects his tumultuous life in the ghetto, while Ludacris focuses on boasting in his high-energy club songs and Nas includes inspirational, thought-provoking themes in his rhymes.

Hip-Hop as a Lifestyle

Hip-hop's influence on popular culture has been immense. It is an integral part of the lives of millions of people in the United States and abroad. Classes on hip-hop culture and on the work of such rappers as 2Pac (later known as Tupac Shakur) and Lil' Kim are taught in a number of major American universities. Rap artists join their rock and roll contemporaries on tour and in performances at major sporting events such as the Superbowl and the NBA All-Star Game. Hip-hop songs are among the most popular ringtones for cell phones, and hip-hop artists contribute to the soundtracks for video games and movies.

But hip-hop has also endured its share of doubters and controversy. In its formative years, hip-hop culture, along with its various manifestations, was dismissed as a fad. Embraced by the young generation, it created a rift with parents who thought that rapping was not music, that graffiti was not art, and that break dancing was not dancing. Furthermore, as rap became popular, its at times negative influence was bemoaned by a number of activists. Feminist groups have denounced the misogynistic lyrics of some rappers, religious figures have criticized the violent, "thuggish" work of gangster rap artists, and civil rights organizations have boycotted several rappers because of their homophobic lyrics.

Despite these detractors, hip-hop has provided a sense of hope and purpose for millions of people. Hip-hop is considered by its practitioners and followers as the voice of the voiceless, the voice of youth, and a major cultural force. Hip-hop has given a generation of people hope that they could become successful and respected in any number of ways, whether by winning a DJ tournament, designing acclaimed artwork, choreographing the dance moves for a music video, starting their own business, or becoming a platinum rapper.

Indeed, Jay-Z, 50 Cent, and Snoop Dogg are part of the select group of artists who are no longer looked at as just rappers. They are now personalities, entertainers who are among the most respected and powerful celebrities in the world. They all had a desire to make it as rappers, to be successful in their lives, and to achieve the American Dream—and they all did it with the musical and cultural force known as hip-hop.

Chapter One

The Roots of Hip-Hop Culture

Hip-hop culture was born in the mid-1970s in the Bronx, an impoverished section of New York City inhabited by a large segment of lower-class African Americans and Latinos. The increasingly poor borough was disintegrating because of crime, arson, housing abandonment, and overall neglect by its residents and their landlords. Many vacant, crumbling, high-rise apartment buildings provided an ideal haven for illegal activities, including drug dealing, robbery, and murder.

Amid this chaos, a group of young black and Latino Bronx residents with few economic resources and a need to express themselves created their own entertainment with the materials available to them. They played the record collections of their parents to entertain themselves, they used the cardboard boxes littering the streets as dancing surfaces, and they used cans of spray paint to make their own art. The result was the birth of a new culture: hip-hop culture.

Hip-hop culture includes rapping, DJing, graffiti art, and B-boying, also known as break dancing. Rappers recite words over music, DJs play records and perform in front of an audience, and break-dancers perform an energetic style of dance that often includes exaggerated body movement and acrobatic moves, such as whirls. One of the earliest ways that hip-hop culture found expression, however, was through graffiti.

Graffiti Style

Though illegal, graffiti became popular in Philadelphia in the 1960s as a way for people to express themselves in public places. By the 1970s, it had spread to New York City. Some graffiti artists, also known as writers, were members of street gangs who wrote their gang names on walls and benches to mark their territory. Other graffiti artists who were not in gangs promoted themselves as artists by creating their own nicknames, or tags, to accompany their drawings. A few paid homage to their neighborhood by including in their tag the number of the street on which they lived. For example, some of the early graffiti artists were Taki 183, Joe 136, Julio 204, and Frank 207.

These graffiti artists often used bright colors to enhance their designs. They wrote their tags in a number of different styles, from basic print or cursive writing to more elaborate fonts that included calligraphy-like designs

Master DJ Afrika Bambaataa plays a record to provide dance music. In the early days of hip-hop, young people would entertain each other by playing records at informal outdoor concerts.

and shading. Regardless of the design, the point of graffiti was for it to be seen, so the artists made sure that the color of the paint they used was visible against the wall or backdrop on which they painted.

Graffiti writers made their biggest mark on the subway trains that traveled throughout the New York metropolitan area. While trains were parked in the train yard at night, graffiti writers went to work painting their exteriors. To the artists, subway cars were large, mobile canvases.

Although graffiti was seen as art by the people doing it, others did not share this view. People living in the wealthier sections of New York City looked at graffiti as a symbol of the decay of their city. People living in graffiti-filled areas bemoaned the art, which defaced buildings and reduced the attractiveness and value of property in their neighborhoods. They also resented the gang members who used graffiti to mark their territory. However, in the desolate Bronx environment, many young people turned to graffiti as a

Graffiti is used by artists to express themselves publicly and by gang members in order to mark their territory.

source of entertainment. They used it not only as a means of self-expression but also, since it was illegal, as a way to rebel against the government that they felt ignored their desperate plight.

Kool DJ Herc Creates a Culture

Most of the graffiti artists had similar musical tastes. By listening to music, they and other young residents of the Bronx could temporarily escape their abysmal surroundings. These residents listened to soul artists such as Al Green and Marvin Gaye, funk practitioners James Brown and George Clinton, disco acts such as Chic and the Bee Gees, and the electronic group Kraftwerk, among many others.

One of these young music fans was Clive Campbell, better known by his stage name, Kool DJ Herc. He was born in Kingston, on the Caribbean island of Jamaica, and grew up listening to ska and reggae music, two energetic musical forms that originated in his homeland. An avid music fan and record collector, Herc (short for Hercules, the Greek warrior hero) was impressed by the sound systems used by disc jockeys (DJs) in Jamaica. DJs are people who play and comment on recorded music, either on the radio, in dance clubs, or at concerts. The DJs that Herc watched as a child transported monstrous speakers and record collections to outdoor concerts given in front of hundreds, and sometimes thousands, of people.

In 1967, when he was twelve, Herc immigrated with his family to the Bronx, bringing his love for music with him. As he grew up, Herc decided he wanted to become a DJ. After collecting enough records and stereo equipment, he began hosting open invitation block parties where he played music to entertain the people. To play the music loud enough, he created a sound system that he modeled after the mobile setups he had heard and seen in Jamaica.

With the help of his friends, Herc carted his enormous speakers, which often stood up to 6 feet (1.8m) tall, and prized selections from his mammoth collection of more than one thousand records to the courtyards of public housing buildings and plugged his equipment into the lampposts. This pilfered electricity powered his turntables and allowed him to play music for the neighborhood for hours. Within months, the parties that Herc hosted drew an increasingly large and diverse group.

Many of the people gravitated to the parties, which were held on a smaller scale in the recreational rooms of apartment buildings, because the events were like going to a nightclub, but the attendees did not have to dress up or pay for admission. The parties were also easy to get to. Some participants could simply walk outside to the courtyard of their apartment building. For others, the parties were only a subway ride away. The events were an easy and convenient gathering point for a group of people with little disposable income and few inexpensive entertainment opportunities, especially for those who enjoyed dancing.

The Breaks

Herc noticed that people who enjoyed dancing at his DJ sessions became especially animated during certain kinds of songs, particularly funk songs when the music would "break" down, having the percussion instruments playing alone. People enjoyed dancing to the breaks more than any other portion of the song. Dancers also used the breaks to showcase specialized dance routines with complicated spinning and leg maneuvers.

With his DJ sessions becoming increasingly popular, Herc made a breakthrough in how a DJ works. He extended the breaks, making them the focal point of his DJ sets. To do this, he put one copy of the same song on each of his two turntables. A device known as a mixer, which DJs normally put between the two turntables to manipulate a record on one turntable without having to reach over the other turntable while it was playing, allowed Herc to switch between the two records. He would find the break on one record, play it, and then switch over to the same break section on the record on the second turntable, using a knob called a fader. Once he had practiced finding the breaks in songs, Herc could repeat them over and over again by using the mixer and fader to shift back and forth

Party Fliers Spread the Word

More than a decade before the advent of the Internet and long before hip-hop events were promoted on television and radio, fliers were the main way to announce hip-hop events to fans. The fliers, handed out in the streets and at other parties or events, provided the address of the club, the evening's host, the time of the party, the performers, and the date.

Famous graffiti artists designed many of the fliers. Initially, the fliers featured the artists' logos or silhouettes. Eventually, photos of the artists, such as the Funky Four, Fantastic Romantic Freaks, Jazzy Jay, Kurtis Blow, and Whodini, were included.

At the end of the 1980s, fliers were sometimes replaced by posters, which were often just larger versions of fliers. These posters were routinely attached to telephone poles, trees, and other objects. Today, fliers preserved by hip-hop fans from the late 1970s and early 1980s are displayed in museums.

between the two copies of the same record.

The dancers at Herc's session loved his breaks. During these extended portions of the rhythm sections of songs, they were able to practice and experiment with moves that before had been limited to brief flashes during the climax of a song. Intricate footwork, spinning moves, and mechanical motion were the signature moves of the dancers. For example, they did headspins by standing on their heads and spinning around with their arms outstretched and legs raised toward the sky. Another was the moonwalk, in which the dancers slide backward as their feet and legs appear to be moving forward.

Herc called these dancers break boys, since they danced to the breaks. The dancers became known as B-boys for short. The early B-boy crews included the Shaka Zulu Kings and the Shaka Zulu Queens. They traveled the Bronx and other parts of New York, going from party to party to showcase their dancing.

Kool DJ Herc influenced early sounds of hip-hop by extending the percussion breaks in the songs he played.

Afrika Bambaataa: Master of Records

The parties that Herc hosted included other DJs besides himself. Among them were Grandmaster Caz (later of the Cold Crush Brothers), Grandmaster Flash, and a young Afrika Bam-baataa, who eventually earned the title of Master of Records because of his immense knowledge of a wide range of musical styles including rock, soul, funk, R&B, and reggae. Besides being a DJ, Bambaataa was also a member of a Bronx street gang called the Black Spades. Eventually, however, Bambaataa came to believe that gang warfare was destroying his beloved city. Gangs sold drugs and killed people,

A DJ uses a device known as a mixer, positioned between two turntables, to combine sounds from two different records.

and Bambaataa believed they had to be stopped. Bambaataa later reflected on the impact gangs were having in New York during the 1970s: "I saw it was time to move the gangs in a different direction, before we all wound up dead or in jail."[1] To do so, Bambaataa formed the Zulu Nation, a peaceful organization that aimed to popularize and promote the developing hip-hop culture. It adopted the motto "Peace, unity, love, happiness, and fun."[2]

Using a pair of turntables his mother had bought him for his high school graduation, Bambaataa quickly established himself as one of the premier DJs of the burgeoning hip-hop culture, with a reputation to rival that of Kool DJ Herc. He used a wide range of records from any musical style he could collect, from the fiery, funky rock music of James Brown to the computerized sounds of Kraftwerk. Bambaataa later became known as the Godfather of Hip-Hop.

Battles Begin as Hip-Hop Parties Grow

With Herc and Bambaataa becoming celebrities in their neighborhoods, competition between DJs began to develop. DJs began unofficial rivalries with each other to see whose sound system was the loudest and whose sets were best received by the crowd. Bambaataa later recalled his early DJ sets:

> I would come with 16, 20 crates of vinyl, and play from 9 till 4 in the morning, switching records every minute or two. We were always trying to outdo each other, play records more obscure than any other deejay, scratching out the titles so other deejays couldn't copy us. People would tell me they didn't like salsa music, but I'd slam some on 'em with a break beat, and they'd be dancing to it. I'd work in calypso and rock, the Monkees, Kraftwerk, James Brown, and just for kicks an old Coke commercial or "My Boyfriend's Back." You came to my shows, you were going on a musical journey.[3]

The high-energy music played by renowned DJs such as Kool DJ Herc and Afrika Bambaataa transformed sets into more than just an opportunity to listen to a smorgasbord of sounds. At these parties people could watch B-boy crews such as the Rock Steady Crew, the most respected B-boy group because it was known to have the best dancers. Besides watching the B-boys perform seemingly gravity-defying dance moves, attendees could associate with the graffiti artists who were literally making their mark on subway trains and buildings throughout the city

or just soak in the atmosphere of the hip-hop scene.

The people attending these gatherings did their own unofficial recruiting by urging their friends, neighbors, and family members to join them at the hip-hop parties. Yet the scene remained largely unknown to the rest of the world.

The Itch to Scratch

DJs remained the stars of hip-hop gatherings, so up-and-coming DJs were eager to find ways to separate themselves from other DJs. In 1975, high school student and aspiring DJ Grand Wizard Theodore developed another asset to help DJs impress audiences. But unlike Kool DJ Herc, who deliberately incorporated elongated breaks into his DJ routine, Theodore created his addition to hip-hop culture by accident and in isolation. His invention: scratching. Scratching occurs when the DJ moves a record back and forth against the needle, creating a scratching sound. In a 2001 interview, Grand Wizard Theodore recalled how he invented scratching:

> I used to come home from school and go in my room and practice a lot and this particular day I came home and played my music too loud and my mom was banging on the door and when she opened the door I turned the music down but the music was still playing in my headphones and she was screaming "If you don't turn the music down you better turn it off"

Afrika Bambaataa formed the Zulu Nation, an organization whose goal was to promote hip-hop music and culture as an alternative to gang activity.

and I had turned down the speakers but I was still holding the record and moving it back and forth listening in my headphones and I thought "This really sounded [like] something [special] . . . interjecting another record with another record." And as time went by I experimented with it trying other records and soon it became scratching.[4]

Grand Wizard Theodore also created the needle drop, an important but often overlooked DJ tactic. The needle drop occurs when a DJ drops the needle on a record at exactly the point he wants the record to play without having to cue it up or listen to it. Theodore did this by looking at the record itself. Records were made out of vinyl. On each side is one long, continuous groove that circles the record dozens of times. When certain musical changes, such as a guitar solo, take place in a song, the spacing between the coils of the groove changes, becoming either wider or narrower. After listening to a song several times, a DJ can look at the vinyl, tell by the spacing where such musical changes occur, and thus know where to drop the needle to play a desired section.

As more and more DJs entered the hip-hop field, they continued to develop, refine, and enhance their routines. The use of breaks, scratching, and needle drops, among other techniques, livened up the DJs' sets. The DJ had evolved from someone who simply played records and worked a crowd to someone who knew how to keep partygoers dancing from the start of the party until the last song was played. As the one in control of the party, the DJ was the center of hip-hop culture, which got its name because of the way the dancers would "hip" and "hop" (jump and move) to the music.

Rappers Emerge

To keep the crowds entertained during breaks in their sets, the DJs hooked up microphones to their sound systems and spoke to the audience. They said simple phrases such as "And ya don't stop" and "To the beat, y'all." But during the sets themselves, the DJs, who had to focus on keeping the party going by playing the right records, had their friends keep the crowd engaged by talking on the microphone. Such a vocalist was called an MC, short for master of ceremony. At first, the main purpose of the MC was to praise the DJ. For instance, an MC might say that Grandmaster Flash "cuts faster" than the competition, meaning that he could cut, or scratch, more effectively and efficiently than other DJs. "Grandmaster cuts faster" also sounded clever because it rhymed. The MC in this instance was thus rhyming and praising Grandmaster Flash simultaneously. The MCs soon became popular attractions and started talking more and more frequently during the parties. They often spoke in rhyme and engaged in call-and-response with their audience. For example, the MC would

Spoken-Word Poets Precede Rappers

At least five years before rappers began to emerge in the Bronx section of New York, a number of politically minded spoken-word poets were reciting their poetry over music. The Last Poets, Gil Scott-Heron, and the Watts Prophets were among this group of performers and are often considered the first generation of rappers. These three acts infused their poetry with political commentary. Their work included condemnation of white oppression, affronts to then-president Ronald Reagan, and championing of the black power movement.

On the other side of the artistic spectrum was a host of rhyming spoken-word artists who favored comedic material. Rudy Ray Moore, known by the self-proclaimed titles Godfather of Rap and the World's First and Only Rappin' Comedian, is best known for his work as the character Dolemite. In 1970, Moore released *Eat Out More Often*, his first comedy record. Its tales regaled listeners with frank discussions of sex. As his comedic career took off, Moore's wild characters and their remarkable adventures and accomplishments earned him a rabid fan base. Blowfly was among those who released albums similar to Moore's in the early 1970s.

Spoken-word poet Gil Scott-Heron is often said to be one of the earliest rappers.

Grand Wizard Theodore (left) and rap pioneer Busy Bee attend a hip-hop awards show. Rappers rose to prominence by helping DJs fill out their music sets.

say to the crowd, "Everybody say 'Ho,'" and those in attendance would respond by yelling "Ho!" This call-and-response created a lively atmosphere, similar to that found in some churches, and made the audience feel as though they were part of the entertainment, not just being entertained. Besides "Everybody say 'Ho,'" the MCs popularized famous sayings such as "What's your Zodiac sign?" and "Throw your hands in the air like you just don't care."

By the late 1970s, the MCs were becoming stars in their own right and were drawing their own crowds. DJs and club and party promoters began pitting aspiring MCs against each other in sharp exchanges of wit called battles. Now, instead of making the DJ the focus of the action by rapping about the joys of partying and the merits of their DJ, the MCs vied for the spotlight against each other. Like the DJs before them, MCs took great pride in being able to entertain crowds and deliver the

Boom Boxes Blast Rap Music

Around 1980, personal stereos became a popular way for people in New York to listen to music while they were outside. These personal stereos, known as "boom boxes" because loud music would boom from the speakers, could easily be carried from one location to the next. They typically received both AM and FM radio stations and had one or two cassette decks. Cassette tapes from early hip-hop events were often played on these personal stereos.

In 1980, only a few rap songs had been released commercially on record and there were no radio shows dedicated to playing rap music. This made the boom box essential in spreading rap music quickly throughout the streets of New York City. Indeed, the mobility of the boom box allowed rap fans to carry it along on the subway, into a store while shopping, or onto a basketball court while watching a game. Radio owners personalized their stereos by adding a strap so they could sling it over their shoulder or by tagging the radio with graffiti.

Boom boxes, like the one held by this man, helped spread rap music throughout New York City in the 1980s.

most memorable rhymes, which often included boasts about their rhyming abilities.

During the MC battles, the art of freestyle rhyming evolved. This kind of rapping is defined by MCs who make up rhymes on the spot. Typically, these clever performers described the room in which they were rhyming, the crowd they were performing for, or the clothing or look of their opponent, which they often criticized.

Hip-Hop Spreads

MCs could use the bragging rights from a battle to land hosting gigs at area clubs and even headline their own shows. Club managers started hiring DJs and MCs, now also called rappers because of the way they would rap (slang for "converse" or "talk") with their audience, because it was clear that they could draw crowds. Some of the early clubs that showcased rap were Harlem World, Disco Fever, and the Rock Steady Lounge. The success of these shows convinced the shrewd entrepreneurs among the DJs, rappers, and club owners that they could sell recordings of the events. Soon, cassette tapes featuring the work of the emerging DJs and rappers in New York City spread across the country.

These recordings allowed listeners to visit a world that had previously been available only by attending a party or a hip-hop night at a club in New York City. Almost as soon as they were made, copies of the cassette tapes were sent, borrowed, and shared with friends and relatives. In this way, DJs, rappers, and fans created hip-hop followers across the country. People were drawn to the new style of music that was typified by breaks and the rappers speaking in rhymes over the music to an energetic audience. Hip-hop was set to graduate from an underground phenomenon into a movement embraced by music executives eager to profit from it.

Chapter Two

Hip-Hop Gains Momentum

As hip-hop culture gained momentum in the New York underground scene, DJs such as Grandmaster Flash and DJ Hollywood and rappers such as Busy Bee and Melle Mel drew hundreds of people to nightclubs. Block parties hosted by Kool DJ Herc, Afrika Bambaataa, and others remained popular gathering places for B-boys, graffiti artists, and aspiring DJs and rappers. Propelled by a host of creative and energetic artists, the fledgling hip-hop culture was one event away from emerging on a national scale. That event was a song.

"Rapper's Delight"

Rap and hip-hop took a major step forward in 1979 with the release of "Rapper's Delight" by the Sugarhill Gang. It was only the second rap song ever recorded and released commercially. (The first was "King Tim III [Personality Jock]" by the Fatback Band.) Sugar Hill Records owner Sylvia Robinson, who had been a successful

R&B singer and songwriter before becoming a record company executive, wanted to record a novelty record she hoped would cash in on the hip-hop trend. She assembled three little-known rappers, Wonder Mike, Master Gee, and Big Bank Hank, and had them record a song. The result, "Rapper's Delight," which borrowed its groove from "Good Times" by the disco group Chic, became a smash hit.

Each rapper contributed simple, playful lyrics that welcomed everyone to the hip-hop world. Early in his first verse, Wonder Mike invited people of all races and nationalities to join the group's musical party. The Sugarhill Gang filled the rest of the song with other themes that many people could relate to: an affinity for flashy fashion, the desire to attract members of the opposite sex, and the awkwardness of having an uncomfortable experience with a friend.

Several future music superstars were among the more than 2 million people who bought a copy of the single. In fact, "Rapper's Delight" was the first record that popular R&B singer Mary J. Blige, who emerged in the 1990s, ever bought. She explains, "It was the newest thing, so everyone was running to get it."[5]

Rap Makes Commercial Strides

"Rapper's Delight" eventually reached No. 36 on the pop singles chart and peaked at No. 4 on the R&B chart. The popular song was for many people their introduction to rap. After all, anyone who did not live in or visit the New York metropolitan area could not experience hip-hop culture firsthand.

The success of "Rapper's Delight" convinced a few record company executives that this new form of music could be profitable. The song demonstrated that this new art form could be mass-produced, bought, sold, and enjoyed on a national scale. Less than a year later, Kurtis Blow became the first rapper to get a recording contract with a major record company when he signed with Mercury Records in 1980. It was a major accomplishment for the genre, which at that time was still a virtually unknown commodity. Another

The Sugarhill Gang first gained attention in 1979 with the song "Rapper's Delight."

breakthrough came in 1981, when the Funky 4+1, a rap group best known for its festive single "That's the Joint," was featured on the hit comedy sketch program *Saturday Night Live*, thereby becoming the first rap group to make a national television appearance.

Most major corporations and media entities, however, ignored rap. They looked at the new form of music as a fad, like disco, that would soon disappear. This lack of interest from corporate America forced rap, much like rock and roll before it, to develop without the influence of major record companies.

"The Message" Strikes a Chord

Sugar Hill Records used the success of "Rapper's Delight" to become a prominent rap label. The Sugarhill Gang followed up the song with the 1980 cut "8th Wonder," which peaked at No. 15 on the R&B charts, and the 1981 single "Apache," which peaked at No. 13 on the R&B charts. But the next landmark release from Sugar Hill Records came from Grandmaster Flash & the Furious Five, a respected rap collective anchored by renowned DJ Grandmaster Flash and rapper Melle Mel. The group released "The Message" on the label in 1982. It became one of the most influential and significant rap singles of all time.

Unlike the few commercially released rap songs that preceded it, "The Message" described the desolate neighborhoods that many members of the

In 1980 Kurtis Blow became the first rapper to get a contract from a major record company.

hip-hop culture called home. It was a dark, somber song that stood in stark contrast to the party music, brimming with braggadocio, that most rappers were releasing at the time.

A number of prominent rappers, from gangster rap pioneer Schoolly D to respected lyricist Common, cite "The Message" as their reason to rhyme. Gangster rapper Jayo Felony recalls the impact that "The Message" and Melle Mel made on his life:

"The Message," that's when I finally really got into writing raps, when I heard that song. Before then, I never really used to hear people cuss on records and at the end of the record, I heard him say, "Get in the goddamn car," and that was like the first time I heard somebody say anything like that and the raps he was talking about were real street. "Don't push me, 'cause I'm close to the edge / I'm trying not to lose my head." That song inspired me to rap.[6]

Rap Style Gets Tougher

In addition to the darker tone of "The Message," people were drawn to the song because the rhymes of Melle Mel were more sophisticated and complicated than those of other rappers such as the Sugarhill Gang or Kurtis Blow. The ascension of Melle Mel gave rap a street edge. Mel was a seasoned veteran of the mid-1970s rap circuit who won a number of rhyming battles be-

cause of his tremendous rhyming talent and his ability to construct complex rhymes. With a commanding voice, riveting rhymes, and an intimidating stage presence, Mel (also known as Grandmaster Melle Mel) was the type of rapper that other rappers aspired to be. He was articulate, clever, tough and, most of all, respected by the hip-hop community.

By contrast, the Sugarhill Gang members—Master Gee, Wonder Mike, and Big Bank Hank—favored a simple pattern that often incorporated obvious rhymes, such as "cat" with "hat" or "feet" and "seat." Other rappers, such as Busy Bee and Kurtis Blow, favored a similarly simple, good-natured, laid-back rhyming approach that could not keep up with the lyrical advance of rappers such as Melle Mel, Kool Moe Dee of the Treacherous 3, and T La Rock, whose multisyllabic words and fast delivery patterns required great skill to perform without stumbling over the lyrics.

The Rap Sound

Even though "Rapper's Delight" was a party record and "The Message" reflected the harsh reality of living in an American ghetto, the two shared a number of similarities. Like most of the rap music from this period, the use of instruments in these songs was minimal. Unlike songs in other genres of music, which included a variety of instruments (sometimes with intricate progressions), rap music of this era typically featured only drums, a bass

DJ Grandmaster Flash was part of a rap group known as Grandmaster Flash & the Furious Five, which released the influential song "The Message" in 1982.

line, and maybe a keyboard effect or two. Unless the songs were recorded with a house band, as was the case with some of the recordings produced by Sugar Hill Records, few other instruments were used.

Part of the reason rap artists used minimal instrumentation was that, as outsiders in the music business, they lacked access to state-of-the-art studios. Instead, they often recorded music in amateur home studios that did not have the capability to produce the type of comparatively complex, layered recording favored by established studios. Therefore, rappers not backed by a house band often did their rhyming over only a drum track that came from a drum machine, a piece of studio equipment that makes a variety of drum sounds that can sound remarkably similar to those produced by a live drummer.

Many musicians and record company executives said that rap, with its sparse sound and style, was not music because its songs did not contain melody, a rhythmically organized sequence of single tones so related to one another as to make up a particular musical passage or idea. In fact, many R&B and funk artists went out of their way in interviews to discredit rap music.

But the criticism did not stop rap from evolving. Afrika Bambaataa's 1981 single with the Jazzy Five, "Jazzy Sensation," set the stage for his landmark work with Soul Sonic Force (the name was also written as Soulsonic Force). Their 1982 single "Planet Rock," which borrowed the melody from Kraftwerk's quirky "Trans-Europe Express," helped pioneer a new sound that relied on keyboards and electronic sound effects to accent the music. Many of these sounds recalled a computer blip or the chirping of birds. Bambaataa and his group rapped and sang much in the way that old funk bands did: intermittently, with computer-altered voices and with long breaks in which the music played uninterrupted. Bambaataa later recalled how he invented his new sound, which he dubbed "electro-funk":

I learned from James [Brown], Sly [Stone] and Uncle George [Clinton]. But I was also listening to Yellow Magic Orchestra, Kraftwerk and Gary Numan, and getting off on the electronic music

Rap artist Melle Mel is widely respected by other rappers for his complex rhymes.

in John Carpenter's *Halloween* movies and *Assault on Precinct 13*. I wanted to be the first black group to come out with that sound. So I formed Soulsonic Force and invented electro-funk.[7]

Hip-Hop Hits the Big Screen

As rap continued evolving with new sounds and styles, graffiti, B-boying, and DJing were also making major contributions to hip-hop culture. The festive video for "Rapper's Delight" featured B-boys showcasing some of their dance moves, while the gritty video for "The Message" took place on a run-down city street with buildings covered with graffiti.

The 1982 film *Wild Style* showed how interwoven and interrelated each component of hip-hop was at that point. The movie had several story

The electric melodies created by the band Kraftwerk (pictured) helped DJs like Afrika Bambaataa pioneer a new sound in hip-hop called electro-funk.

Graffiti as Opera

In Martha Cooper's book Hip Hop Files: Photographs: 1979–1984, Style Wars *director Tony Silver recalls how he was introduced to the graffiti lifestyle that he depicted in his landmark film:*

My original idea for what became *Style Wars* was a short film about a b-boy crew. . . . Henry [Chalfant, *Style Wars* codirector] and I talked and I saw his photos, which were amazing, and I got more and more excited about a larger film that would have a number of elements and music. The problem was the subject seemed so big; it was hard to envision the shape of it. One night, Henry and I and Kathy, his wife, were talking about the movie. Kathy, who is an actress, went into this riff, this aria, "You have to understand how dramatic this is. You are going to a scary train yard in the middle of the night, you have a bag of cans, you're hanging off the side of a train painting a mural in just one night that will cover the whole side of a subway car. And any minute you'll be chased by the cops." To me, it sounded like an opera. You risk everything to go to the edge, a struggle for recognition against all odds, not some made-up story—but an opera that's real.

lines, among them the struggle that a graffiti writer goes through to balance his personal life with his love for his art. The movie featured graffiti writers, rappers, DJs, and B-boys in prominent roles, giving attention to each segment of the flourishing hip-hop culture. *Wild Style*, the first authentic and earnest look at the culture, is considered the definitive hip-hop movie.

Much as cassette tapes and "Rapper's Delight" had done a few years earlier, *Wild Style* gave many people their first exposure to hip-hop. But *Wild Style* was especially significant because it provided a visual look at the culture. Now, people could emulate the graffiti artists, rappers, and B-boys they saw on screen, allowing hip-hop to grow quickly in the underground and also leading to the 1983 graffiti film *Style Wars*.

B-Boying Takes Center Stage

While rap was looked at with skepticism by the mainstream business world, B-boying was the first element of hip-hop culture to be embraced by corporate America. Released in 1983, the smash film *Flashdance*, starring Jennifer Beals as an aspiring ballet dancer, also featured Crazy Legs, Mr. Freeze, and Prince Ken Swift, members of the seminal B-boy group Rock Steady Crew.

The next year, *Breakin'* hit movie theaters. The film centered on a jazz dancer and two B-boys who team up and become popular street dancers. Television commercials, endorsements, and other deals soon followed for B-boys who had garnered media attention from their film and in-person performances. Today hip-hop documentary film producer and one-time professional B-boy QD3 recalls the impact of B-boys: "B-boying was the first thing that drew attention to hip-hop, period. It was really the spark that made it go mainstream. Before that it was contained. *Flashdance* came out and break dancing was the bridge that we crossed to go into the rest of the world to some degree. [Break-dancers] were the first superstars."[8]

Rap Gets Media Expsoure

As B-boying and graffiti were enjoying commercial exposure, rap was making strides of its own. By October 1983, both Mr. Magic and Kool DJ Red Alert, prominent DJs in the hip-hop community, had radio shows on the New York airwaves. These shows, the first commercial radio outlets to showcase rap music, were critical in spreading the genre throughout New York and the country. A person who had never heard a rap song could now turn on the radio and hear entire programs dedicated to rap. In fact, many of Mr. Magic and Kool DJ Red Alert's radio shows were recorded and shared among rap fans, much like the recordings of early rap performances.

Also in 1983 came the debut of Video Music Box. Entrepreneur Ralph McDaniels of Brooklyn, a section of New York City, hosted the video music show, which was shown on public television and at the time was the only program showing hip-hop videos. The first video the program aired was "5 Minutes of Funk" by rap trio Whodini.

The breakthrough of rap on radio and video provided the perfect platform for Kurtis Blow. On his 1984 hit "Basketball," the good-natured rapper cleverly wove the names of basketball stars such as Dr. J and Moses Malone into his rap about his love for the sport. The video for the song, which featured Blow rapping on a basketball court, was one of the early examples of a rap song that garnered considerable attention from those not in the hip-hop audience.

With all elements of hip-hop culture making their mark in society, rappers started touring, particularly in Europe, where the culture was openly embraced. In 1982, Afrika Bambaataa organized the first European hip-hop tour. He later recalled his world vision for hip-hop: "I was taking music from all over the planet to spread this new sound all over the planet. I wanted to break it in the Tri-State area, then across the U.S.A. and then the world. I

The 1984 movie Breakin' *featured B-boys and helped popularize break dancing.*

had a vision that this was more than just party music for the ghetto."[9]

DJs and Rappers Emerge from Hip-Hop

As DJs, rap songs, and rap artists began to enjoy more and more success in the mid-1980s, graffiti and B-boying became little more than gimmicks to corporate America. Graffiti was still illegal, and even though some graffiti artists were commissioned, they had to paint in a controlled, often indoor environment that removed the thrill of the

Kool DJ Red Alert had one of the first radio shows featuring rap music.

larity. Instructional break-dancing tapes were sold on television, making it seem as though anyone who bought the tapes and a dancing mat could be an instant B-boy star. As with other skills, it took years of practice for B-boys to perfect their moves. But companies eager to cash in on the break-dancing trend portrayed these extraordinary dance skills as easy to acquire.

Although break dancing became common in mainstream culture, rap was still an art form on the fringes. Major labels had yet to fully embrace the new music, allowing independent record companies such as Sugar Hill, Jive, Reality, Profile, and Tommy Boy to corner the rap market. These small companies, free to pursue any artists they deemed worthy without having to worry about approval from a corporation, signed a variety of rap talent that reflected the diverse range of people who made up the hip-hop community.

The rap trio Whodini, for example, wrote creative, narrative raps about social outcasts and love that were performed over keyboard-driven music, while Doug E. Fresh showcased his beatboxing skills on a number of his early recordings. Beatboxing is the art of using the mouth to create percussion sounds that serve as a beat for someone else to rap to. Beatboxing enjoyed exposure in several 1980s movies, including the comedies *Police Academy* and *Disorderlies*, which starred the rap group Fat Boys.

forbidden, as well as the rebellious edge of the art.

As the art world started looking elsewhere for cutting-edge work, B-boys also started losing some of their popu-

But the breakout group of this era was Run-D.M.C. This trio from Queens, a borough of New York City, featured rappers Run and D.M.C., and DJ Jam Master Jay. The first release from the group was the seminal 1983 single "It's Like That/Sucker MC's." The group presented itself as common guys on the street who had much in common with their fans. Run, who later became an ordained minister and changed his name to The Reverend Run, recalls, "One big part of Run-D.M.C.'s success was our catchy rhymes that made you think or sometimes laugh. No violence or harsh language, just thinking, laughing, and having fun."[10]

Other Musicians Embrace Hip-Hop

As Run-D.M.C. helped expand rap's commercial base in the late 1970s and early 1980s, musicians who appreciated the grassroots nature of rap also embraced the emerging music, giving it some credibility in the musical community. Deborah Harry rapped on "Rapture," a 1981 single from her rock group, Blondie, in which she mentioned hip-hop celebrity Fab Five Freddy (also written as Fab 5 Freddie) and used the hip-hop slang word *fly*, another way to say that someone or something was "cool." Jazz musician Herbie Hancock teamed with Grandmixer D.ST (who later changed his

The members of Run-D.M.C. wear trademark gold chains at a 1987 performance.

Gold Chains Become Prized Possessions

In the mid-1980s, gold-plated chains became one of hip-hop's most prominent fashions. Besides being a fashion statement, the chains were a status symbol that signified that the rapper was accomplished, because the chains were expensive and most people living in the New York ghettos where the rappers were raised could not afford them. Nicknamed "rope chains" because many of them were thicker than rope, these gold chains were worn by nearly every rapper of the era.

Many rappers wore one rope chain. But several rap acts, including Eric B. & Rakim and Big Daddy Kane, took the trend a step further by wearing several chains at once. No rapper, though, made gold chains as prominent as Slick Rick, the playful storytelling rapper who wore so many chains that people wondered why he did not tip over because of the weight.

As gold became common, it fell out of favor in the early-1990s and rappers looked for another jewelry fashion statement. They found one in platinum chains, which took the place of the gold rope chains.

name to Grandmixer DXT) for the 1983 hit "Rockit." The video for that song featured D.ST scratching and was the first time most people saw a DJ performing a scratch. R&B singer Chaka Khan featured Melle Mel on her 1984 single "I Feel for You," marking the first time that an established R&B singer collaborated with a rapper on a single.

Each of these singles gave different audiences an opportunity to experience hip-hop culture when paired with a type of music they already enjoyed. Music fans no longer had to seek out rap. It was popping up in a variety of other music styles. With rock, jazz, and R&B musicians embracing it, rap and, by default, hip-hop culture were slowly increasing in visibility and influence. As it continued developing and enjoying more and more success, rap music started earning coverage in mainstream publications such as rock magazine *Spin* and the *Village Voice*, a respected New York–based weekly newspaper. With its artists pushing themselves creatively and more and more independent record companies releasing rap songs, the genre was ready for its next big step.

Chapter Three

The Golden Era of Rap

By 1984, rappers including Run-D.M.C., Kurtis Blow, Whodini, and Fat Boys were popular enough to mount the landmark Fresh Fest Tour, the first national rap tour. These lyrically advanced acts had replaced the call-and-response and rhymers of the 1970s. Other than Run-D.M.C., however, this set of acts was itself about to be replaced during the golden era of rap, the years from approximately 1986 to 1989.

During this period, rap enjoyed an explosion in the range, skill, and talent of rappers. Rappers focused on a variety of lyrical topics and presented themselves in a variety of guises, representing virtually every segment of society: hippies, gangsters, party people, political activists, lovers, materialists, poets, and lyrical enthusiasts. Indeed, rappers of this era went well beyond the elementary party rhymes that the first and second generations of rappers had often employed, crafting ingenious raps about everything from dating to government corruption.

Rap Replaces Hip-Hop Culture

As rap enjoyed a creative explosion during the golden era, the other three components of hip-hop culture began to fade from the spotlight, especially B-boying and graffiti. Although both survived, they were marginalized by rappers and, to a lesser extent, DJs.

The DJ was still a prominent part of live performances who provided input on the music. But for the first time, the other elements of hip-hop were used merely to supplement the rapper. For example, there might be a set of B-boys dancing in a rap video, but they were no longer the focal point. Rappers and the music they were producing were now taking center stage.

Sampling Becomes Prominent

In the early years of rap, artists such as the Sugar Hill Gang, Grandmaster Flash & the Furious Five, and Kurtis Blow often rapped over live instrumentation

Run-D.M.C. remained popular during the mid- to late-1980s while other early rappers were replaced by a new generation of artists.

that borrowed guitar rhythms, bass lines, and drum patterns from other songs, including, most famously, the Sugar Hill Gang's usage of Chic's "Good Times" for "Rapper's Delight."

Following this habit of duplicating other artists' music, rap producers in the golden era of rap began "sampling" other songs, a practice that would permanently alter the direction of rap. Sampling occurs when a portion of a song from another recording is copied onto a piece of studio equipment called a sampler, which allows the original piece of music to be used on a new record. It is literally a sample, or portion or segment, of the original song. By using this technique, the rappers and their producers no longer needed to have musicians

Samples Bring Lawsuits

The media hype surrounding the violent lyrics of gangster rappers and the sexually explicit raps of 2 Live Crew made rap a magnet for controversy, thereby exposing the music to more listeners, some of whom purchased the music simply out of curiosity. But some of these new consumers, who had grown up listening to rock and roll, had one purpose while listening to rap music: to find illegal samples contained in a song.

Sampling became a simple procedure for rap producers as soon as the practice was popularized in the mid-1980s. But since sampling required using other people's music, it made rappers easy targets for copyright infringement lawsuits by the owners of the songs that were being sampled. 2 Live Crew, targeted because of the graphic sexual content of its breakthrough 1989 album, *As Nasty as They Wanna Be*, was sued by the estate of Roy Orbison over the group's usage of the music of the rock icon's "Pretty Woman." Biz Markie, a successful, lighthearted rapper, saw his career grind to a near halt in 1991 when he was sued for sampling Gilbert O'Sullivan's "Alone Again Naturally" without permission. Biz's *I Need a Haircut* album was subsequently pulled from record stores, emphasizing to producers the potential consequences of sampling a song without first getting permission.

Rapper Biz Markie's career was seriously hobbled when he was sued for illegally sampling music.

actually play music in order to make a song.

Samples typically last from four to eight measures, but they can also be shorter or longer, depending on the wishes of the artist or producer. The samples are often matched with a drum pattern, also potentially sampled, that fits the same tempo. In addition to samples of music, samples of singers, speeches, sound effects, and other noises and sounds are used. For instance, the screeching of soul singer James Brown was a favorite sample of early rap producers.

Run-D.M.C. Walks To Superstardom

Run-D.M.C. was one of the major beneficiaries of the idea of sampling. The group's third album, 1986's *Raising Hell*, became a multiplatinum success thanks in large part to the song "Walk This Way," a collaboration with rock group Aerosmith. Run-D.M.C. originally planned on sampling the guitar riff Aerosmith had used on its song of the same name a decade earlier. But at the behest of producer Rick Rubin, Run-D.M.C. contacted Aerosmith and eventually performed with guitarist Joe Perry and singer Steven Tyler on "Walk This Way."

With "Walk This Way," rap and rock created common ground that garnered the interest of fans of each genre. The video for "Walk This Way" marked a watershed in rap's development, as it was played in heavy rotation on the music video channel MTV. For many

people not already interested in rap, "Walk This Way" was the rap song that they enjoyed, and the video gave them their first taste of hip-hop fashion. Run-D.M.C. had been developing its look, which featured black hats, black jeans, black jackets, gold chains, and white Adidas sneakers without shoelaces, for years.

Another *Raising Hell* single was "My Adidas." Here, Run-D.M.C. paid homage to its favorite shoe and, in effect, identified itself with the brand. Musician and producer Sean "Diddy" Combs, a Run-D.M.C. fan, recalls seeing the group perform when he was a kid. "I was at the Raising Hell Tour at Madison Square Garden [in 1986], and Run-DMC held up their Adidas and told everybody in the crowd to hold up their Adidas," he says. "I swear, 20,000 people held up their sneakers. I remember I was like, 'I wanna do that one day.'"[11]

LL Cool J Makes Rap Sexy

The music of Run-D.M.C. was mostly gritty, aggressive, and bombastic, typical of rap music at the time. Even though the group had a sizable female following, some women found rap too abrasive, loud, and unrefined. Many women felt as though no rapper was speaking to them.

LL Cool J filled that void by catering to women in some of his music and soon became rap's first sex symbol. His debut album, 1985's *Radio*, was better known for such rugged selections as "I Can't Live Without My Radio," "Rock

Run-D.M.C. Dress Hip Hop

In his spiritual memoir, It's Like That, *The Reverend Run explains the significance of the fashion that Run-D.M.C. introduced:*

How we dressed was just as innovative as our sound. Run-D.M.C. pioneered a whole new way of dressing. We would have on sweat suits and black hats and unlaced Adidas. It was funny how we got that look. [Group member Jam Master] Jay was responsible for our dress code.

It was around 1984 and we were making money, and Jay bought whatever he wanted. One day Jay wore this incredible outfit. He was walking down Jamaica Avenue, the main shopping drag in Queens, and he had on all this expensive stuff: leather pants and a leather jacket, Adidas, a big gold rope, a black hat, and some Gazelle glasses. Everybody was checking him out, because he had on everything that everybody else wanted. (Jay could afford everything because we were making fifteen hundred to two thousand dollars for every

performance. And we were working hard for the money. We could do two shows in Brooklyn and two shows in Queens and Yonkers all in the same night if we started around 7:00 p.m. and things were scheduled right.)

You might see somebody with a rope or some Adidas or some Gazelles but not every one of them on at the same time. Jay was walking down Jamaica Avenue and it was like everybody wanted to snatch something from him because he had it going on. I mean nobody had everything: the glasses, the leather, the shoes, and the gold rope. So we were doing well and Jay just was helping to create a nationwide trend and didn't know it.

[My brother] Russell later refined the look by matching everything up so the appearance was cool but neat. But it was Jay who first influenced our look.

When the albums blew up [became popular], so did our look. Almost every young person in America tried to emulate us in some way.

the Bells," and "I Need a Beat" than its songs geared to women, "Dear Yvette" and "I Want You." With the release of "I Need Love" two years later, however, LL Cool J was established as a ladies'

man. After all, his name stands for Ladies Love Cool James.

LL Cool J endured criticism from the rap community for making hip-hop love songs. Many of his detractors felt

LL Cool J became rap's first sex symbol, targeting female fans by introducing love songs to the world of hip-hop.

that, by making love songs, LL Cool J was diluting rap, making the genre soft and taking away its edge. Nonetheless, his albums also contained several harder-edged hip-hop songs that appealed to rap fans of either gender eager to hear his clever braggadocio rhymes and aggressive beats. By taking a creative risk, LL Cool expanded rap's lyrical scope and almost single-handedly brought rap a new wave of female fans.

Female Rappers Make Their Mark

During the golden era of rap, when LL Cool J was rising to stardom, the previously male-dominated rap genre experienced an explosion of female talent. Much as LL Cool J had done, these female rappers increased rap's fan base and expanded their reach by making music that was not as abrasive and confrontational as that of their male counterparts.

Salt 'N Pepa (sometimes spelled Salt-n-Pepa) became the first female rap stars. Rappers Salt and Pepa and rapper/DJ Spinderella, who joined the group after the release of its breakthrough debut album, 1986's *Hot Cool & Vicious*, had a string of hit singles that gave female rappers credibility. The dance song "Push It" became a party favorite, while "Tramp" trashed two-timing men and "I'll Take Your Man" displayed the women's seductive side. For the first time, a female rap group was respected. Writer Stephen Thomas Erlewine explains in AMG All Music Guide:

As the first all-female rap crew (even their DJs were women) of importance, the group broke down a number of doors for women in hip-hop. They were also one of the first rap artists to cross over into the pop mainstream, laying the groundwork for the music's widespread acceptance in the early '90s. Salt 'N Pepa were more pop-oriented than many of their contemporaries, since their songs were primarily party and love anthems, driven by big beats and interlaced with vaguely pro-feminist lyrics that seemed more powerful when delivered by the charismatic and sexy trio.[12]

MC Lyte, another credible female rapper, broke through in 1986 with the impassioned "I Cram to Understand U" single, which was part love song, part antidrug parable. In her subsequent material, MC Lyte rapped about everything from the damaging impact of drugs and her rapping ability to having fun and being in love, showing that female rappers could rhyme about a variety of topics with lyrical skill equal to their male counterparts. "From the very beginning, I knew that there are many different sides to me," Lyte says. "In recording the very first record, it was OK to be vulnerable on record. It was OK to talk about your feelings and I just respect that in anybody in the craft that can do it. OK, you're the best at what you do and that's great, but then also have other things going on that you don't mind discussing."[13]

MC Lyte is the first female rapper to earn a gold record, for her single "Ruffneck."

The Brooklyn-reared artist is the first solo female rapper to earn a gold single, for 1993's "Ruffneck." In a genre quick to dispose of its pioneers, she has maintained her status as one of the most respected female rappers of all time, a performer who was embraced for her rapping talent, not just her looks. "She's a good-looking female, don't get me wrong, but it wasn't the sex that was selling it," says platinum rapper Fabolous, who was also

raised in Brooklyn. "When she got on the microphone, she was spitting like a dude, like a real MC. That definitely caught my eye back in the day."[14]

Rappers as Poets

As Run-D.M.C., LL Cool J, and female rappers earned more and more attention from newspapers and magazines that had not previously covered rap in much detail, other rappers of the golden era were becoming more and more proficient, creating increasingly complex and detailed rhymes that used complicated rhyme schemes and imagery. The artists, their followers in the streets, and even a few journalists started considering rappers poets, a step that signaled that rappers were now being taken seriously by the media. For instance, in the 1992 essay "Poets with Attitude," published in the *Washington Post*, University of Minnesota and Macalester College teacher Alexs Pate referred to specific rap songs from as early as 1987 to argue that rappers were aware of the poetic process and engaged in literary expression.

Three of the most respected rappers of this era, and the ones who arguably possessed the best poetic and story-telling abilities, were Rakim, Slick Rick, and Big Daddy Kane. Unlike most other rappers, who favored energetic deliveries, Rakim rapped in a laid-back but commanding tone that made him sound like an authoritative scholar, respected and worthy of being emulated. Rakim and his partner and DJ Eric B. released *Paid in Full*, their debut album, in 1987. The poetic power of Rakim is evident on the song "I Know You Got Soul," in which he raps about becoming one with the paper on which he writes his rhymes.

Whereas Rakim was typically serious, London-born rapper Slick Rick first garnered attention in 1985 as MC Ricky D through his work with Doug E. Fresh & the Get Fresh Crew on their songs "The Show" and "La Di Da Di," both of which featured Rick's creative storytelling ability and his humorous outlook on life. In 1988, Slick Rick released his dynamic debut album, *The Great Adventures of Slick Rick*. Resembling a series of short stories set to music, the album featured Slick Rick taking listeners on journeys that were cautionary ("Children's Story"), inspirational ("Hey Young World"), and wistful ("Teenage Love"). Rick also had several sexually explicit songs that detailed his relationships with women, but the racy content did not detract from Rick's storytelling skill.

Rakim had poise and Slick Rick had humor, but Big Daddy Kane was possibly the most well-rounded rapper of the golden era of rap. The Brooklyn-bred rapper established himself as a tough-talking artist whose lyrical prowess dazzled hardcore hip-hop followers and whose rugged good looks made him attrac-

tive to women. His first two albums, 1988's masterful *Long Live the Kane* and 1989's *It's a Big Daddy Thing*, showcased one of Kane's biggest strengths: his diversity. He was equally adept when rhyming about his lyrical ability ("Raw," "Ain't No Half-Steppin'"), instilling pride and hope in

Rap artist Rakim is respected for his poetic lyrics and commanding delivery.

the hopeless ("Word to the Mother [Land]," "Another Victory"), imagining a better world ("I'll Take You There"), or seducing women ("I Get the Job Done," "Smooth Operator"). As rap journalist and editor Reginald C. Dennis wrote in the liner notes of *The Very Best of Big Daddy Kane* in 2001,

Describing Big Daddy Kane's place in hip-hop history is like pondering the accom-

plishments of Miles Davis or Muhammad Ali. Both were incredibly powerful presences, even without Miles playing a note or Ali stepping into the ring. Their energy—a near mystical aura of attraction—could be felt from a single black-and-white photograph. And in the end what they did wasn't as important as how they did it. They were just vessels for the truth—and the

Big Daddy Kane performs in 1989. Big Daddy Kane, known for his masterful rapping skills, remains a hip-hop icon.

truth, as we all know, is magnetic. And so was Big Daddy Kane.[15]

An artist conscious that his music had an impact on his followers, Kane made a point of including political and social messages in his music, giving his poetry a purpose. "I thought that I needed to do that for the simple fact that people listened to what I say," he said. "I wasn't one of those artists where people throw my song on and just dance to it. People actually listened to the lyrics. Because of that, I thought that that [having messages in my music] was something that I should get across."[16]

Rap Gets Political

Indeed, rappers during the late 1980s were mindful that their words could have an impact on their listeners. Bronx rap group Boogie Down Productions (BDP) released the confrontational *Criminal Minded* in 1987 and, after the murder of group member DJ Scott LaRock, the politically minded *By All Means Necessary* the following year. The album featured powerful songs about the need for peace, the impact of political corruption, and the importance of safe sex.

BDP helped create a brand of rap later labeled "conscious rap," which incorporated political and social commentary and often advocated armed revolt against the government and other agencies that the artists considered oppressive. The movement also included Brand Nubian, X-Clan, and Poor Righteous Teachers. The most popular and arguably the most influential group of the conscious rap movement, however, was Public Enemy. After releasing the sizzling *Yo! Bum Rush the Show* in 1987, the group released a year later what many music critics consider the best rap album of all time, *It Takes a Nation of Millions to Hold Us Back*. As writer Stephen Thomas Erlewine writes in AMG All Music Guide:

Public Enemy rewrote the rules of hip-hop, becoming the most influential and controversial rap group of the late '80s and, for many, the definitive rap group of all time. Building from Run-D.M.C.'s street-oriented beats and Boogie Down Productions' proto-gangsta rhyming, Public Enemy pioneered a variation of hardcore rap that was musically and politically revolutionary. With his powerful, authoritative baritone, lead rapper Chuck D rhymed about all kinds of social problems, particularly those plaguing the black community, often condoning revolutionary tactics and social activism. In the process, he directed hip-hop toward an explicitly self-aware, pro-black consciousness that became the culture's signature throughout the next decade. Musically, Public Enemy were just as revolutionary as their production team, the Bomb Squad, creating dense soundscapes that relied on avant-garde cut-and-paste

Chuck D (left) and Flavor Flav of Public Enemy perform in 1990. Though highly entertaining, the group was best known for its politically charged lyrics.

techniques, unrecognizable samples, piercing sirens, relentless beats, and deep funk. It was chaotic and invigorating music, made all the more intoxicating by Chuck D's forceful vocals and the absurdist raps of his comic foil Flavor Flav. With his comic sunglasses and an oversized clock hanging from his neck, Flav became the group's visual focal point, but he never obscured the music.[17]

The Native Tongues

Whereas Public Enemy, BDP, and others had a militaristic bent to their politically infused music, the rap collective Native Tongues (whose members included Jungle Brothers, De La Soul, A Tribe Called Quest, and Queen Latifah, among others) put more playful and inspiring, but less confrontational messages in its music. The members of the collective promoted peace, justice, and equality, but their music made it clear that they were willing to enjoy themselves in the meantime.

Although each member of Native Tongues was important, De La Soul had the greatest impact on rap's development, especially with its first album, 1989's *3 Feet High and Rising*. De La Soul changed the composition of rap albums via its pioneering use of humorous skits, which were interwoven into the flow of *3 Feet High and Rising*. These skits were not songs, but interludes that featured group members participating in a humorous game show. Today, virtually every rap album has at least one skit.

In addition to Native Tongues, other New York rap groups were making tremendous creative strides. Gang Starr, for instance, was one of the first rap groups to incorporate jazz music into its work, while Stetsasonic called itself the "hip-hop band" because it used live instruments during its recordings and performances, something unheard-of in the era of sampling. The comical and controversial Beastie Boys demonstrated for the first time that white rappers could create quality rap music respected by members of the

Pictured performing in 1996, A Tribe Called Quest was part of the Native Tongues music collective that promoted peace and justice with their works.

The Beastie Boys Get "Ill"

The Beastie Boys were among rap's first bad boys. Signed to the legendary Def Jam Records, the trio of Mike D, MCA, and Ad-Rock got its start in the early 1980s making punk music. But they soon turned their attention to rap and in 1986 released their first album, the controversial and hugely successful Licensed to Ill. *Writer Stephen Thomas Erlewine explains the album's impact in the AMG All Music Guide:*

An amalgam of street beats, metal riffs, b-boy jokes, and satire, *Licensed to Ill* was interpreted as a mindless, obnoxious party record by many critics and conservative action groups, but that didn't stop the album from becoming the fastest-selling debut in Columbia Records' history, moving over 750,000 copies in its first six weeks. Much of that success was due to the single "Fight for Your Right (to Party)," which became a massive crossover success. In fact, *Licensed to Ill* became the biggest-selling rap album of the '80s, which generated much criticism from certain hip-hop fans who believed that the Beasties were merely cultural pirates. On the other side of the coin, the group was being attacked from the right, who claimed their lyrics were violent and sexist and that their concerts—which featured female audience members dancing in gogo cages and a giant inflatable penis, similar to what the [rock group Rolling] Stones used in their mid-'70s concerts—caused even more outrage. Throughout their 1987 tour, they were plagued with arrests and lawsuits, and were accused of inciting crime.

Mike D, MCA, and Ad-Rock (left to right) of the Beastie Boys pose in New York City in 1987.

rap community. Nonetheless, Beastie Boys was treated by some critics and rap fans as a novelty act because its members were white and used juvenile humor in their music.

Rap Expands Beyond New York

White rappers were not the only ones looking to join the rap world. In the late 1980s, after the success of Run-D.M.C., LL Cool J, Salt-n-Pepa, Beastie Boys, and several movies depicting hip-hop culture, rappers from cities besides New York began making their own brands of rap music. Artists from these other cities experimented with sound, rap style, and lyrical content, continuing rap's creative development and adding new elements to the genre.

In Philadelphia, DJ Jazzy Jeff & the Fresh Prince, the good-natured rap duo whose playful songs "Parents Just Don't Understand" and "Nightmare on My Street" were quality examples of profanity-free rap, demonstrated that the genre did not have to be confrontational. In Los Angeles, King Tee delivered a California interpretation of New York's braggadocio style of rap, while MC Shy D helped put Atlanta on the map with his up-tempo party raps.

Each of these non–New York acts helped develop the rap scene in its own region, allowing rap to expand quickly throughout the country. With successful rappers now spread across the country, a major rap revolution was about to take place.

Chapter Four

Gangster Rap

As the golden era of rap, with its celebratory, braggadocio, and political emphasis, came to an end in the late 1980s, a new kind of rap was ready to take center stage. This more explicit and more profane brand of rap would become known as gangster rap. In the early days of gangster rap, rappers who performed it presented themselves as street documentarians, artists who reported on life in some of the roughest and poorest ghettos in America. Unlike rap from the golden era, which tended to have an optimistic, boastful bent, gangster rap was confrontational and even scary to some listeners.

Gangster rap featured violent lyrics along with sexually explicit themes that many critics and activists said demeaned women. It created a firestorm of controversy that led to courtroom battles and boycotts. The more explicit the material, the more attention it received.

Schoolly D Lays the Groundwork

Inspired by the gritty raps of Melle Mel on "The Message," aspiring Philadelphia rapper Schoolly D decided in the mid-1980s to take a similarly harsh approach with his music. Schoolly D made the first gangster rap songs, profanity-filled selections in which he rapped about smoking marijuana, having sex with women, and carrying and using guns.

At this time, rap was still in its developing stages and record companies were unsure of the genre's potential to sell enough units to make releasing rap albums worthwhile. Schoolly D recalls that no record companies were interested in his early music:

> I had made this demo in around '83, '84, called "Gangster Boogie." I made one pressing of it and I took it to a disc jockey by the name of Lady B. She told me that no record company was going to

sign it because I was talking about weed [marijuana] and guns. After that, I knew that nobody was going to sign it. So I thought that if [rap businessman] Russell Simmons was a rapper, he'd do his own label. And he said [in an interview] that, "If I was a rapper like my brother [Run-D.M.C.'s Run], I would just do my own label." So I just said, "[I'll do it myself]." They didn't even want to hear clean rap, so I just started doing little things here and there to save up the money to press up my own records. I was part of a [local rap] crew anyway, so I knew everybody in every [Philadelphia record] shop, like Funk of Martin, Sound of Market. All the record stores said that if I pressed the record up, they'd sell them. So I did it.[18]

Launched in 1983, his Schoolly D Records was the first artist-owned rap label. In the next few years, Schoolly D enjoyed regional, but not national, success. His hits included the thunderous "P.S.K. 'What Does It Mean'?" about his Philadelphia gang of violent friends, and the story-driven "Saturday Night" about his wild, violent sexual adventures on Saturday nights. After Schoolly D became an underground sensation, Jive Records signed him to a recording contract and released several of his albums.

As Schoolly D was becoming one of the most talked-about rappers in the streets of Philadelphia, rappers from other cities started making equally controversial and abrasive music. Oakland rapper Too $hort reported on the lifestyle of pimps and prostitutes over slow, bass-heavy music; Los Angeles rappers Ice T and Toddy Tee rapped about the violent, gang-infested streets of their city over spare beats; and the

Gangster rap pioneer Schoolly D got his start as a DJ. Here he spins records at a Philadelphia rave in 1997.

Houston collective Geto Boys brought vivid violence to the forefront with its aggressive production. In New York, rapper Just Ice and rap duo Boogie Down Productions were also releasing music with violent overtones that included explicit lyrics about sex and drugs.

Straight Outta Compton Makes a Mark

As gangster rap was gaining momentum, Eazy-E and N.W.A appeared with music that would galvanize the rap world. Eric "Eazy-E" Wright was a small-time drug dealer and aspiring record executive who revolutionized both the rap record business and the lyrical direction of the music with releases from his record company, whose roster included Eazy-E himself and his flagship group N.W.A, whose other members were Dr. Dre, Ice Cube, MC Ren, and DJ Yella.

The first Eazy-E album, *Eazy Duz It*, and the first N.W.A album, *Straight Outta Compton*, both released in 1988, were full of profanity and got virtually no radio or video play. With violent, jarring music that contained an unprecedented combination of humor, misogyny, and political insight, N.W.A rapped in explicit and articulate terms about the violence and drugs consum-

Controversial rap group N.W.A is known for explicit lyrics concerning violence and police abuse in urban ghettos.

ing its California communities. According to the *Washington Post*, N.W.A "weren't the first rappers to do songs about crime, guns and gang violence, but they heightened the mayhem and the profanity to an unprecedented, nearly surreal degree."[19]

Gangster Rap Gets Attacked

As exciting as its music may have been, N.W.A also made a mark by berating the police for abusing innocent blacks in the ghetto on *Straight Outta Compton*. Law enforcement officials did not appreciate the antagonistic material. In 1989, N.W.A received a now-famous letter from the FBI warning it against releasing songs that advocated violence against law enforcement, while a number of police organizations decided not to provide security at N.W.A performances. The members of N.W.A were arrested and later acquitted of obscenity charges in Cincinnati and had their albums seized in England because they were deemed obscene.

The controversy, along with a string of brilliant but brutal albums, drew fans to the music of Eazy-E and N.W.A, which was more polished and accessible than that of earlier gangster rappers thanks to the crisp, driving production from Dr. Dre and DJ Yella. Their violent music and public appearances catapulted Eazy-E and N.W.A to rap superstardom.

The Geto Boys was another gangster rap act that was targeted because of its violent lyrics. The release of the Hous-

ton group's self-titled 1990 album was delayed when Geffen Records decided not to distribute the record, claiming it glamorized violence and graphic sexual imagery. Soon after, Geffen Records terminated its agreement with subsidiary Def American Records, which had signed the Geto Boys, citing a growing difference in creative philosophy.

In addition to enduring the wrath of law enforcement agencies and record labels unwilling to release potentially controversial material, gangster rappers found themselves under attack from journalists, who criticized the celebratory, one-sided view of violence that gangster rap portrayed. In an article titled "Rap's Hostile Fringe," *Washington Post* writer David Mills explains how the music of gangster rappers failed to provide an even, realistic portrayal of violence in the streets:

> The hard-core street rappers defend their violent lyrics as a reflection of "reality." But for all the gunshots they mix into their music, rappers rarely try to dramatize that reality—a young man flat on the ground, a knot of lead in his chest, pleading as death slowly takes him in. It's easier for them to imagine themselves pulling the trigger.[20]

Other writers noted that the animosity toward women and the rationale for the violence depicted in the lyrics of gangster rap songs were becoming increasingly sensational and without political overtones. *Baltimore Sun* pop music critic J.D. Considine wrote, "It's hard to excuse raps that present women not as people but as orifices, that offer gunplay and physical violence not as a fact of life but as a viable means of settling scores, and that suggest that attitude is a reasonable compensation for a sense of self-worth.[21]

Gangster Rap as Expression

One of the most common accusations leveled at gangster rap was that it would encourage people to commit violence. Rappers did not agree, arguing instead that their music was a crucial expression of pain and outrage. "A record can't make nobody do anything," N.W.A's MC Ren told *Newsweek* in 1991. "Sometimes doing a record is just my way of getting back, 'cause when [police] got you jacked up on a car, and they got a gun to your head, you can't say s---. Doing records I can speak out. When people listen to the record, that's their way of speaking back."[22]

Another rapper who "spoke out" through his music was Ice Cube, who left N.W.A and started a solo career in 1990. His work often depicted the pain caused by society's seeming indifference to the suffering of blacks in ghettos across America. In his review of Ice Cube's *AmeriKKKa's Most Wanted*, the *Washington Post*'s Mills noted, "After the mad burst of gunshots in the one-minute drama 'The Drive-By,' the voice of a newscaster is heard: 'Out-

side of the South-Central area, few cared about the violence because it didn't affect them.' Ice Cube clearly wants to be more than scandalous."[23]

As time went on and the shock value of gangster rap began to fade, more people began to understand the political messages sometimes contained in the music. In fact, some music critics began to write about the prophetic properties of gangster rap. Several critics noticed that the rage and sense of injustice contained in the work of N.W.A foretold the riots that ensued after four white police officers were acquitted in the videotaped beating of black Los Angeles motorist Rodney King. The *Washington Post* staff writer Richard Harrington, for instance, wrote, "In the wake of the Los Angeles riots, the media belatedly recognized that rap, in the tradition of vanguard political art, had for several years provided an early warning system that didn't wake up a slumbering and inattentive bureaucracy until it was too late."[24]

LL Cool J, one the most respected members of the hip-hop community, also recognized the significance of gangster rappers:

I listen to the politicians and activists blame rap for everything under the sun, from world violence to world hunger. But if you removed every rapper from the face of the earth, you'd still have violence and wars. In fact, if not for certain rappers, "mainstream" society would have no idea of

Body Count Controversy

With N.W.A, 2 Live Crew, and the Geto Boys drawing the ire of the police and political activists, it was clear that rap music was a polarizing topic.

In 1992, Ice-T created further controversy with the song "Cop Killer," even though it was sung by his offshoot rock and roll group Body Count and was not a rap song at all. The song, which Ice-T sang from the perspective of someone who kills police officers, was protested by police activist organizations. Even though Ice-T shouted and sang his lyrics and did not rap them, he and the entire rap genre were blamed for advocating violence against law enforcement. Writer Stephen Thomas Erlewine explains in his biography of Ice-T on the AMG All Music Guide Web site:

Body Count proved to be a major turning point in Ice-T's career. On the basis of the track "Cop Killer"— where he sang from the point-of-view of a police murderer—the record ignited a national controversy; it was protested by the NRA [National Rife Association] and police activist groups. Time Warner Records initially supported Ice-T, yet they refused to release his new rap album, *Home Invasion*, on the basis of the record cover. Ice-T and the label parted ways by the end of the year.

Rapper Ice-T experienced a turning point in his career with the release of the inflammatory song "Cop Killer."

Gangster rap artist Ice Cube performs solo in 1992.

what is going on in our communities, where real war is being waged every day. For many Americans, life is rough, and gangsta rap was born out of that misery, pain, and hunger. It didn't create it.[25]

California Becomes a Hip-Hop Hotbed

But gangster rap did create something signficant: a new business opportunity for gangster rappers. The success of Eazy-E and N.W.A had record labels scrambling to find their own gangster rapper and led to a wave of artists from Compton, the tough Los Angeles suburb that N.W.A put on the national radar. After N.W.A came Compton acts DJ Quik and Compton's Most Wanted.

A multitude of other talented, gangster-inspired rap groups from Los Angeles, including the smooth Above the Law, the political WC and the MAAD Circle, and the pro-marijuana Cypress Hill, soon became hugely successful as they focused on the harsh reality that ghetto residents often faced. Suddenly, profanity, violence, and sex were what the record companies clamored for, helping make gangster rap the most popular and promoted style of rap.

Even though this new wave of California gangster rap acts was celebrated by rap fans, detractors viewed the groups as exploitative. "One group dares to call itself Compton's Most Wanted, capitalizing on that area's reputation for gang violence, a reputation made international by N.W.A's platinum album *[Straight Outta Compton]*,"[26] Mills wrote.

Gangster Rap's New Sound

The tension that gangster rap depicted soon appeared within gangster rap groups themselves. Ice Cube left Eazy-E's company in 1989 because of a financial dispute. Dr. Dre later departed

Eazy-E, also over money issues. In early 1992, Dr. Dre released "Deep Cover," a single from the soundtrack of the movie of the same name that introduced new Dr. Dre protégé Snoop Doggy Dogg, who also rapped on the song.

Snoop Doggy Dogg (today known as Snoop Dogg) was a lanky, laid-back rapper from the Los Angeles suburb of Long Beach. His slick raps and relaxed rhyme style struck a chord with rap fans. The release of "Deep Cover" established Snoop Dogg as a promising new talent and signaled the triumphant return of Dr. Dre. But it was the release of the first Dr. Dre solo album, *The*

The California hip-hop group Cypress Hill raps about drug use and ghetto violence in its songs.

Pop Rap from L.A.

Even though Los Angeles gangster rappers were the obvious beneficiaries of the success of Eazy-E and N.W.A, the momentum created by their popularity also allowed non-gangster Los Angeles rap acts to earn a chance in the spotlight. Pop rapper Tone-Loc broke through in 1989 with his infectious smash singles "Wild Thing" and "Funky Cold Medina," two catchy tunes that contained a winning mix of captivating plotlines and humor. Soon thereafter, Young MC, who wrote lyrics for Tone-Loc, scored his own hits with the party song "Bust a Move" and a humorous look at school mischief, "Principal's Office."

Even though Tone-Loc and Young MC were quality artists with solid albums, the rap industry considered them pop acts, mere novelties that did not truly represent what rap was really about: the streets that gangster rap portrayed.

As writer Stephen Thomas Erlewine explains in his review of Young MC's Stone Cold Rhymin' *album on the AMG All Music Guide Web site,*

Young MC wasn't given props [respect] at the time and he wasn't respected in the years following the release of his debut *Stone Cold Rhymin'* largely because he worked entirely in the pop-rap/crossover vein. All the same, that's what's great about his debut, since it's exceptionally clever and effective, a wonderful combination of deft rhymes and skillful production.

Chronic, at the end of 1992 that made both Dr. Dre and Snoop Dogg, who was featured prominently on the album, superstars.

Whereas the music Dr. Dre produced for N.W.A was simmering with rage, the music on *The Chronic* contained a heavy funk influence, which resulted in a more laid-back, musical sound that was easier for a wider range of people to digest. Still, however, the lyrics written by Dr. Dre, Snoop Dogg, and other guests, including future rap stars Kurupt and Daz Dillinger, contained the same type of violent imagery and profanity that just a few years before had bothered governmental agencies, music critics, and fans.

Thanks in part to the censorship battles and critical backlash N.W.A and the Geto Boys faced, Dr. Dre and *The Chronic* were not met with the kind of heated, repeated protests that earlier gangster rap was. Those battles had already run their course, clearing the way for mainstream outlets such as *Rolling Stone* magazine and MTV to embrace gangster rap as a form of legitimate music. This acceptance was a turning point for rap. For the first time, rap music commanded attention because of the quality of the music not because it was a fad, a gimmick, or something controversial. In fact, in 1997, *Rolling Stone*, considered the premier rock and roll magazine, listed *The Chronic* as one of the 200 albums on its Essential Rock Collection list. In the review of the album that accompanied the list, music critic Lorraine Ali said, "*The Chronic* changed the sound of hip-hop

and R&B, and its effects, both positive and negative, resonate through '90s pop culture."[27]

2 Live Crew Gets "Nasty"

While N.W.A, Snoop Dogg, the Geto Boys, and other rap groups took violence as their theme, 2 Live Crew created controversy by rapping about sex in explicit terms. The group recorded dozens of songs that contained profane descriptions of sex acts. In 1990, the Miami rap group's *As Nasty as They Wanna Be* album, its third, was pulled from record store shelves in several states, including Florida and Maryland, after government officials asked retailers to restrict sales of the album to adults. Some record stores then went a

Rappers Snoop Dogg (left) and Dr. Dre perform in New York City in 1999.

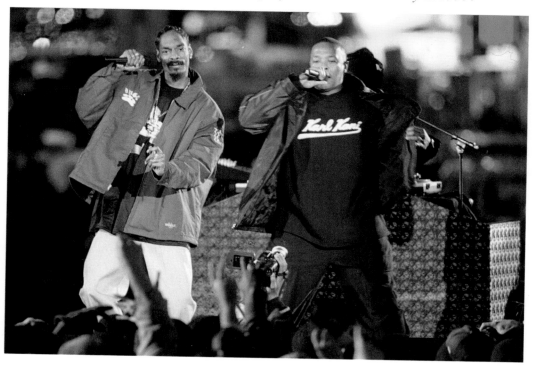

A record store owner displays 2 Live Crew's controversial album, As Nasty as They Wanna Be. *Many music stores refused to carry the album when it was released.*

step further by removing all 2 Live Crew recordings from their stores.

In June 1990, a U.S. District Court judge in Florida ruled that *As Nasty as They Wanna Be* was obscene, and two of the four members of 2 Live Crew were arrested after performing songs deemed obscene. However, in October 1990, a Florida jury, claiming to view the lyrics as art, acquitted 2 Live Crew of performing obscene material. The case drew national attention to the legal debate about freedom of speech and the difficulty of defining what is and is not deemed obscene.

National publications covered the 2 Live Crew obscenity trial, and once it was over, some people defended the group's music. "Clearly this judgment should serve as notice to others trying to find music obscene that Americans believe very strongly in our First Amendment rights," Trish Heimers, speaking on behalf of the Recording Industry Association of America, told the *Washington Post.* "Whether they find it vulgar or obnoxious or lewd still does not mean that it is criminally obscene."[28] Other commentators, however, took a harsher view. The *Washington Post* columnist Jonathan Yardley wrote,

The recording is filth, pure and simple, utterly devoid of socially or artistically redeeming qualities.

"As Nasty as They Wanna Be" is to all intents and purposes one uninterrupted barrage of lewd and scatological language, a monotonous recitation of all the standard-issue four-letter words and numerous others of greater length; it is—yes—witless, strident, insulting to even the dullest intelligence and, above all else, contemptuous of women. It is beyond the powers of my imagination to conceive that it could bring pleasure to anyone, though apparently it does.[29]

New York Embraces Gangster Rap

N.W.A, 2 Live Crew, and Dr. Dre earned as much media exposure as rap had ever experienced to this point, if not more, yet the rest of the rap community was not necessarily happy about the rise of the gangster rap scene, especially in Los Angeles. New York rappers initially dismissed the gangster rap of the West Coast as unimaginative, pointless, and not "real" hip-hop because it lacked the lyrical complexity that had blossomed during the golden era of rap. New York rapper Tim Dog even recorded a song criticizing the entire city of Compton and dedicated his debut album, 1991's *Penicillin on Wax*, to attacking the artistic merit of Los Angeles–based rappers.

Still, as Eazy-E, Dr. Dre, Snoop Dogg, and other rappers became more popular than any other rap acts, their style influenced a legion of New York rappers, including Kool G. Rap & DJ Polo, the Beatnuts, Mobb Deep, and Fat Joe, all of whom infused their music with a gritty feel that showed the direct influence of the confrontational material of Eazy-E and N.W.A. Even so, East Coast rap's distaste for the rapid rise of the West Coast led to an understated bitterness between the two primary rap cities. New Yorkers did not view the West Coast artists as legitimate, and the Los Angeles artists resented this lack of respect. The competition led to an explosion of rap as a business.

Chapter Five

The Rap Business Explodes

As rap's popularity and cultural influence continued to expand in the early 1990s, rap music became increasingly controversial and violent. But another crucial development was also taking place: The rise of gangster rap created a new generation of artists who became astute businessmen. They started their own record companies and had the power to sign artists and dictate how money was going to be spent to promote them, making rap's financial stakes bigger than ever.

Eazy-E Changes the Rap Business Model

Like Schoolly D before him, Eazy-E decided to start his own record company in the 1980s. His Ruthless Records released a few singles through local record distributors and enjoyed modest success, but Eazy-E wanted national exposure. A visionary who dreamed of becoming a music industry mogul, he had no interest in running a record company whose artists were popular only in Southern California. So he and his manager started shopping his music and that of N.W.A to major record labels.

Eazy-E was rejected by several of these labels, which were not interested in doing business with an unproven rap record executive. But Priority Records, an independent company that had released a number of rap compilations, was interested in the graphic, shocking music that Eazy-E and N.W.A recorded. So, at a time when no rap artist from the West Coast had made a national impact, Ruthless Records signed a production deal with Priority Records for albums from these rappers. Ruthless had to deliver albums from N.W.A and Eazy-E, and Priority was responsible for the distribution of those records and the implementation of Ruthless's marketing plan, which included pushing the potentially frightening image that Eazy-E and N.W.A had guns and were not afraid to use them.

The rest of the imagery N.W.A used was equally important, as it created a style that was easily identified as that of West Coast rappers. The members of N.W.A often wore dark sunglasses (which Eazy-E later sold through order forms in Ruthless Records albums) and all-black clothing featuring the logos of the Los Angeles Raiders and Los Angeles Kings sports teams. Eazy-E and Ice Cube also wore jheri curls, a hairstyle popular among black men in Los Angeles that was identified by loose curls and a shiny appearance.

Like Run-D.M.C. before them, the N.W.A rappers inspired a generation of kids to follow their fashion lead. Los Angeles radio personality Julio G explains the appeal of Eazy-E:

> He was really that street person that people relate to because everybody knows a guy like him. In the hood, everybody knows that dude. Even when you look at his pictures, it just signifies and shows you a lifestyle and an era of Los Angeles that he represented. He represented a lot of people that were like that with the jheri curl and the hat.[30]

Even though Ruthless and Priority Records had little music industry

West Coast rapper Eazy-E worked to focus national attention on a rap style and image that started in Southern California.

Bone Resurrects Ruthless

As Death Row Records became the prominent West Coast rap label, Eazy-E and his Ruthless Records faded from the spotlight. Eazy-E rebounded by branching out of Southern California and signing Cleveland rap group Bone thugs-n-harmony, who popularized the tongue-twisting rap style introduced in the early 1990s by Twista, then known as Tung Twista. Below is an excerpt from Jason Birchmeier's biography of the Cleveland group in the AMG All Music Guide:

Graced with a quick, sometimes sung delivery, Bone thugs-n-harmony burst out of the Midwest in the mid-'90s with a pair of massive hits ("Thuggish Ruggish Bone" and "Tha Crossroads") along with a great album (*E 1999 Eternal*) and then quickly unraveled. Eazy-E signed the group—initially comprised of Krayzie Bone, Wish Bone, Flesh-N-Bone, Layzie Bone, and Bizzy Bone—to Ruthless Records and released a debut EP [extended play], *Creepin*

on ah Come Up (1994). The EP boasted "Thuggish Ruggish Bone," a conventional G-funk [gangster funk] song with an unconventional array of Bone Thug rappers that became an overnight summer anthem, especially throughout the Midwest. Amid the fervor, the Cleveland rap group entered the studio immediately and emerged with a remarkable album, *E 1999 Eternal* (1995). The album topped the charts and spawned a pair of popular singles, "1st of the Month" and "Tha Crossroads," the latter a Grammy Award recipient. . . . As was in vogue at the time, the group members pursued respective solo careers and also a Mo Thugs Family spin-off group.

Cleveland rap group Bone thugs-n-harmony helped Eazy-E and Ruthless Records expand beyond Southern California.

muscle, once Eazy-E and N.W.A were promoted nationally, both their music and their look become wildly popular. Eazy-E's *Eazy Duz It* and N.W.A's *Straight Outta Compton* sold more than a million copies each. At the time, that was an astronomically high figure for an independently released rap album.

Ruthless Sets a Precedent

Virtually overnight, rappers became more than artists: They became businessmen who controlled the direction and vision of the music and the artists who recorded for their companies. "What Rosa Parks did for the civil rights movement, Eazy-E did for hip-hop," says Phyllis Pollack, a publicist who represented Eazy-E and some of the artists at his Ruthless Records. "He kicked the door open. I know right now everybody claims to have a label, but Eric was the first hip-hop artist to really make this work on the level that he did."[31]

Rap artists, often looked down upon by corporations and executives who did not view rap as music, could now put their records out themselves, market themselves as they saw fit, and still sell millions of copies, as Eazy-E had demonstrated. "He made a mark and set a blueprint for people to follow in the business," says Eazy's widow, Tomica Wright, who today runs Ruthless Records. "He took something that was looked upon in a negative sense, invested money in the idea and brought it to where people paid attention and wanted to listen to what he and his [artists] had to say."[32]

The success of the Eazy-E and N.W.A albums indeed changed the music community's mind, and Eazy-E soon signed distribution deals for his other artists with a variety of record companies, including major ones such as Atlantic and Epic. The success of Ruthless Records made an impression on a generation of future rappers. Layzie Bone, a member of the multi-platinum and Grammy Award–winning rap group Bone thugs-n-harmony, was signed to Ruthless. Layzie Bone, who with Bone thugs-n-harmony has its own Mo Thugs Records label, recalls,

He showed us that you can be more than just a rapper. If it wasn't for Eazy-E, there probably wouldn't have been any Master Ps [the rapper whose No Limit Records was among the most successful rap record companies in the late 1990s] or Roc-A-Fellas [the company co-founded by Jay-Z]. All of them are patterned off of what Eazy-E did. He showed them everything, how to own your masters, be in control of your company and get the bulk of your money. He showed us how to be executives and really get paid as opposed to being [just] an artist. He really started the real level of taking an independent major.[33]

Rappers Transition to Movies

With rappers now focusing on business as much as their music, many of them began realizing their moneymaking potential. Appearing in a movie or a commercial, for instance, was widely seen as selling out in the first decade or so of recorded rap music, as the movies and commercials of that time typically cast rappers in shallow, stereotypical roles. But both business-minded rappers looking to increase their exposure (and bank accounts) and movie studios looking for new ways to attract people to movie theaters realized in the early 1990s that rappers could be major box office draws.

Almost a decade after the release of such rap-inclusive films as *Flashdance* and *Breakin'*, the movie studios started casting rappers, most of whom had no formal acting training or experience, in leading roles for major motion pictures. Most of these films and television programs featured rappers in roles that required little acting and for the most part mirrored their rapping personas. Lighthearted duo Kid 'N Play launched the successful *House Party* franchise in 1990. Ice-T, who appeared in 1984 in *Breakin'*, scored a starring role as a police officer in *New Jack City*, an acclaimed film that also featured cameos from hip-hop figures such as Flavor Flav and Fab 5 Freddie. Ice-T infused his character with a toughness and swagger that matched his recording personality. Ice Cube also made a successful transition into film with the acclaimed *Boyz N the Hood* in 1991, playing an inner-city Los Angeles teen lured by the guns and violence surrounding him.

Will Smith, better known by his rap name The Fresh Prince, became a television star in 1990 thanks to his leading role in *The Fresh Prince of Bel-Air*. In this show, Smith played a fun-loving, mischievous teen who moves to the affluent Los Angeles suburb of Bel-Air to avoid the pitfalls and temptations of his native Philadelphia streets. Smith, however, took a major gamble in 1993 when he portrayed a gay hustler who befriends a rich white couple in *Six Degrees of Separation*. The impressive performance helped establish Smith as a credible actor and led to his being cast in the 1995 action film *Bad Boys* with comedian Martin Lawrence and the 1996 action blockbuster *Independence Day*, which catapulted him to movie superstardom.

Death Row Records Emerges

With many rappers selling millions of albums with their own companies and others gradually becoming box office stars, the stage was set for a rap company to become one of the most dominant forces in the popular music business. The creative force behind this new company already had a history of making provocative, popular music.

In 1991, bodyguard and aspiring music industry mogul Marion "Suge" Knight, reportedly through threats of violence, got Dr. Dre out of his recording contract with Eazy-E and Ruthless Records. Knight and Dr. Dre teamed to form their own company, Death Row Records, which released Dr. Dre's solo album, *The Chronic*, in 1992.

The success of the album established Death Row Records as one of the most powerful rap record companies in the country. The next Death Row Records release was *Doggystyle*, the first album from Snoop Dogg. It debuted as the No. 1 album in the country upon its release in 1993, making Snoop Dogg the first new artist ever to have an album enter the pop music charts at No. 1. After less than two years in business, Death Row Records thus had the respect of the music industry and the best-selling album in the nation.

Bad Boy Entertainment Is Born

While Death Row Records was dominating the rap market, New Yorker Sean "Puffy" Combs (today known as Diddy) was making plans to enter the rap world as a label head, too. An established music producer, Combs in 1993 formed Bad Boy Entertainment and landed a distribution deal with industry powerhouse Arista Records. The deal ensured that all Bad Boy releases would be available at record stores worldwide.

The next year, Bad Boy Entertainment became an industry powerhouse itself when it released the epic debut album *Ready to Die* by The Notorious B.I.G. Formerly known as Biggie Smalls, the stocky Brooklynite possessed tremendous rapping skill. His wordplay was witty, his vocabulary

Rapper Will Smith, initially known as The Fresh Prince, became one of the first hip-hop artists to star in network television shows and movies.

was vast, his delivery was flawless, his timing was impeccable, his voice was commanding, and his song concepts were innovative. *Ready to Die* made perfect use of all of these talents and gave New Yorkers a gangster rapper from their own area to champion.

Equally important was that *Ready to Die* was a New York (or East Coast) interpretation of gangster rap. Unlike most East Coast rappers before him, B.I.G. infused his music with the edge, paranoia, and rage that filled the best

Bad Boy Entertainment CEO Sean "Diddy" Combs works from an office in New York.

gangster rap albums. As a storyteller, B.I.G. depicted himself in a variety of volatile situations, making his album a journey through the New York rap underworld, just as Eazy-E and N.W.A had taken listeners on similar trips through Los Angeles a few years earlier.

In "Warning," for example, B.I.G. rapped about being hunted down for his wealth, while on "Gimme the Loot" he was the one doing the robbing. "Juicy" documented his rise from average ghetto resident to hip-hop star, and in "One More Chance" he boasted in a devilishly clever manner about his

sexual prowess and his ability to juggle relationships with a number of women. Then, on "Big Poppa," B.I.G. rapped over a smooth, keyboard-driven beat that had the same slow, relaxed feel of much of the Los Angeles rap of the time. By contrast, the New York rap generally featured heavy drum patterns, braggadocio rhymes, and aggressive delivery styles.

Rivalry Between Death Row and Bad Boy

The differences between New York and Los Angeles rap became a point of contention among rap fans. Furthermore, with rap releases now regularly debuting as the No. 1 album in the country and rap albums routinely selling millions of copies, rap became the focus of an unprecedented amount of media coverage. To many of those in the rap community, the attention meant that the stakes were higher and that they would do whatever was necessary to be considered the best. Rap had become more than just music or a way for people to express themselves. It was now big business, requiring a constant struggle by the artists and the companies to which they were signed to stay at the top.

The two rap labels earning most of the accolades during this period were Death Row Records and Bad Boy Entertainment. In 1995, a rivalry between the two companies (and eventually between the West Coast and East Coast styles of rap) was officially born.

At the *Source* Awards, an event held in New York by the industry-leading publication to celebrate rap, Death Row's Suge Knight addressed the audience, several of whom were rap artists. He urged rappers and singers who did not want company CEOs appearing on their songs and in their videos to sign with Death Row Records. The comments were aimed at Bad Boy's Diddy, who was getting a reputation for appearing on songs and in videos of his artists. Diddy was criticized for this because it appeared as though he was

trying to steal the spotlight for himself. When he appeared on stage later in the show, Diddy downplayed any animosity Knight intended. Nonetheless, in a show of support for the East Coast, the New York crowd later booed Death

Brooklyn native The Notorious B.I.G. performs in California in 1995.

Row's Snoop Dogg, who felt disrespected by the outpouring of hostility. The fallout from this event led to a deadly rap rivalry.

2Pac Joins Death Row Records

With tension building between Death Row Records and Bad Boy Entertainment, and between East Coast and West Coast rappers, Death Row Records added a controversial West Coast artist to its roster. Embattled rap star 2Pac, who had released three hit albums and also delivered acclaimed appearances in a number of films, was serving time in prison for sexual assault. Eager to regain his freedom, in

Rap Magazines Create Controversy

In November 1994, 2Pac was shot five times in the lobby of Times Square's Quad Recording Studios in New York. At the time, mainstream media was still relatively reluctant to give rap much coverage, so hip-hop periodicals, notably *Vibe* and the *Source*, ran with the story. In a series of back-and-forth exchanges, conveniently spread from one issue to the next, urban music magazines fanned the flames of what would eventually be called the East Coast/West Coast beef.

In the April 1995 issue of *Vibe*, 2Pac accused his former friend the Notorious B.I.G., Bad Boy founder Sean "P. Diddy" Combs, and others of involvement in his shooting at the New York studio. *Vibe* editors did not attempt to corroborate these slanderous statements, nor did they get in touch with B.I.G. for comment in the issue. They did catch up with him in enough time to write a separate story on him. By this time, 2Pac was suddenly unavailable.

2Pac was busy trying to defuse the growing East Coast/West Coast beef in his own way. In addition to singling out the people he had problems with on his incendiary "Hit Em Up," the rapper was also working on the *One Nation* album with a number of East Coast rappers, including Big Daddy Kane and Nice & Smooth, in an attempt to show that his disagreements were with specific individuals, not an entire region. The rap media, though, did not run with that story.

1995 2Pac agreed to sign to Death Row Records if it would expedite his release from prison. Death Row obliged and overnight 2Pac became the star of the label.

2Pac had been shot in a New York recording studio in 1994 and, in a series of interviews with the national media, had accused both Diddy and the Notorious B.I.G. of involvement in the shooting. 2Pac's accusations further strained the already tenuous relationship between Bad Boy and Death Row artists and established 2Pac as a star who was willing to speak his mind, regardless of whom he might offend and regardless of the consequences.

Like his public statements, 2Pac's music was equally noteworthy. He rapped freely about things that made him happy, sad, and upset, often in profane outbursts followed by thoughtful reflection. 2Pac was a performer that many fans could identify with because of his willingness to share his pain and confusion. He did not put himself above his followers. Instead, he was just like them, struggling to find his way in an increasingly complicated world. Young Noble, a friend of 2Pac and a member of the rap group Outlawz, explains how he and his group have been influenced by 2Pac:

He was our teacher as far as all this [music business]. We watched him. We'd be on the way to the studio and there'd be something

West Coast rappers Snoop Dogg (left) and 2Pac attend the MTV Music Awards in 1996.

that would happen and he's putting it in a rap, right there on the spot. To me, that's what music is about, experience. When you make music like that, it lasts forever. That's why some people would rather listen to some oldies than what's out now. It's timeless when it comes from the heart if you do it right. We're trying to make music like that.[34]

As important as 2Pac's music was, he also changed rap in other ways.

2Pac Shares His World

Although 2Pac gained his greatest celebrity by making gangster rap music with minimal social commentary, his earlier music contained substantial social and political commentary, as well as uplifting messages. In the book Tupac: Resurrection 1971–1996, *edited by Jacob Hoye and Karolyn Ali, the rapper explains why* Me Against the World, *released while he was incarcerated, was his favorite album.*

Me *Against the World* was really to show people that this is an art to me. That I do take it like that. And whatever mistakes I make, I make out of ignorance, not out of disrespect to music or the art. So *Me Against the World* was deep, reflective.

It was like a blues record. It was down-home. It was all my fears, all the things I just couldn't sleep about. Everybody thought I was living so well and doing so good that I wanted to explain it. And it took a whole album to get it all out. I get to tell my innermost, darkest secrets. I tell my own personal problems.

It's explaining my lifestyle, who I am, my upbringing and everything. It talks about the streets but it talks about it in a different light. There's a song on there dedicated to mothers, just a song I wrote just for my mother. And it digs deeper like that. I just wanted to do something for all the mothers. I'm proud of that song. It affected a lot of people.

2Pac was particularly proud of his album Me Against the World.

Through his aggressive videos, 2Pac became the model for what a rapper was supposed to act and look like. 2Pac's music became, in effect, secondary to his celebrity and his image. That image included acting like a *thug* (which 2Pac applied to himself) and wearing bandanas, something Los Angeles gang members were also famous for doing.

2Pac, already upset with the Notorious B.I.G. and Diddy, was more than happy to oblige when Suge Knight asked him to berate both B.I.G. and Diddy at every opportunity. This allowed him to release the rage he felt toward them, and also earned him millions of followers.

2Pac Wages War

In the fall of 1995, 2Pac released the single "California Love," a duet with Dr. Dre that marked 2Pac's first release on Death Row Records. The song quickly became the biggest rap song of the season and set the stage for the February 1996 release of his first Death Row Records release, the double album *All Eyez on Me*.

But it was the 2Pac single "Hit Em Up" that had music fans in a frenzy. In this confrontational tune, 2Pac leveled bone-crushing insults at B.I.G. and the rest of the Bad Boy roster, claiming, among other things, that 2Pac had had sex with B.I.G.'s wife. 2Pac also passed the microphone to his friends the Outlawz, who in turn proceeded to vocally pummel B.I.G. and his crew. "Hit Em Up" stands as one of the most stinging songs in rap history and certainly one of the most popular.

But as Death Row became more popular and embraced violence, it lost its creative musical edge. Dr. Dre, for one, did not condone the increasingly hostile Death Row environment and later in 1996 left the label he had cofounded. 2Pac was not able to leave the label on his own terms. At the peak of his rivalry with B.I.G. and Bad Boy, 2Pac was shot and killed in Las Vegas in September 1996. The murder remains unsolved. Just six months after 2Pac's death, the Notorious B.I.G. was shot to death in Los Angeles.

The deaths of 2Pac and the Notorious B.I.G. put a dark cloud on the hip-hop industry. With these murders, rap had gone from reporting about violence in the early days of gangster rap to creating and becoming part of the violence itself. Nonetheless, the increasing success of rap music gave a multitude of artists across the country hope that they could become rap's next stars.

Chapter Six

The Rise of the South and of the DJ

In the spring of 1997, rap was reeling from the loss of two of its biggest stars, 2Pac and the Notorious B.I.G. The deaths of these two artists brought gangster rap an abundance of notoriety. The genre was again viewed by media pundits as an exclusively negative form of music, and some record companies looked to sign safer, less confrontational artists. One by-product of this shift in attitude was a new focus on two other groups of hip-hoppers: southern rappers and DJs.

Both rappers from the South (and to a lesser degree from the Midwest) and DJs had been marginalized by rappers in New York and Los Angeles and the major recording companies located in these cities. Nonetheless, they had developed their own followings, with different levels of success. The South became the hottest breeding ground for rap in the mid- and late 1990s, while DJs developed a sizable following for their own work.

The Rise of Southern and Midwestern Rap

As rap emerged as a cultural power, more people wanted to participate. For a three- or four-year period beginning in about 1995, artists with divergent sounds and lyrical approaches started making rap music in such cities as Atlanta, Memphis, Houston, and New Orleans. In each city a specific and identifiable sound emerged that was distinguishable from the rap music coming from other cities. These distinguishing sounds led to an increasing regionalism in rap, as many fans stopped listening to music from other areas and supported artists from their own city, who used the same slang and rapped about local issues that mattered to them.

For example, the southern artists in particular rhymed over either energetic beats or beats that used the same soulful feel as the music used in 1970s blacksploitation films. (These low-budget films featured predominantly black casts at a time when blacks had few roles in major motion pictures.) Southern rappers also expanded the types of deliveries that rappers employed and the nuances of the raps themselves. OutKast, for instance, did not hide its southern twang in its raps, as other southern rappers had done before.

Indeed, a pivotal release for southern rap was *Southernplayalisticadillac-muzik*, the 1994 debut album from Out-Kast, the Atlanta duo consisting of Andre 3000 (also known as Dre) and Big Boi. The album resonated because for one of the first times in rap history, a rap act from the South did not copy or imitate the sound and style of established rappers from the East or West. Rather, the duo embraced its Atlanta

Andre 3000 (left) and Big Boi, the members of the Atlanta hip-hop duo OutKast, featured a distinctive sound, separate from both East and West Coast rap.

roots, used southern slang in its raps, and rapped about the black experience in the South. Bubba Sparxxx, a rapper from rural Georgia, remembers the impact *Southernplayalisticadillacmuzik* had on his life:

It inspired me when I heard *Southernplayalisticadillacmuzik.*

. . . Those were *Southern* Black boys, like the kind I went to school with, the kind I knew, the kind my closest neighbor was. They were people that talked like me, they were like people I played football with. So I could just relate more to that story. I had dabbled around writing raps, and I

The West Coast Fades

After ruling rap from the late 1980s to the mid-1990s, the West Coast quickly faded from hip-hop prominence as southern rappers started dominating in the late 1990s. In this October 2004 interview with the author, rapper Yukmouth, of the platinum rap duo the Luniz, from Oakland, California, gives his opinions on why West Coast rap is no longer on top of the rap industry:

I think it's mainly because of the gangbanging [gang activity]. I respect gangbang; it's real serious. But the Bay is unified. We don't gangbang. I can always call E-40, Too $hort, any of them and we're going to do the song. But compared to LA, I can't call Dr. Dre, Snoop, none of them. A lot of LA rappers can't call them, either. It's a difference out here and that's because of the gangbang-

ing that people can't come together because too many family, relatives and friends done died over it. People can't let go. But for us to get to the next level, we're going to have to let that go. Put it to the side. Let's squash all that beef and get some money together. That's how the West is going to win. It ain't going to be one artist, one producer that makes beats. It's going to be a unity thing. When 2Pac was alive, we were proud to be from the West Coast 'cause Pac had it unified. Pac had E-40, Too $hort, Dru Down, Daz, Kurupt, Richie Rich, C-Bo, Rappin' 4-Tay. He had New York rappers on his music, too. That's why Pac did it so tight. He unified the West and that's why his *All Eyez on Me* album is diamond [has sold more than 10 million copies]. You've got to unify to make a statement.

was like 16 or 17, and I said, I really think I can do this.[35]

Other rappers also saw the South as a fertile ground for new rap expression. Suave House, an independent Houston rap label, released hugely successful albums from Eightball & MJG, and LaFace, a label backed by Arista, set up shop in Atlanta and signed OutKast and the Atlanta rap group Goodie Mob.

Despite the achievement of this wave of southern artists, rappers not located in New York and Los Angeles still had a hard time getting people to take their music seriously. Chingy, a party rhymer from St. Louis best known for his 2003 hits "Right Thurr" and "Holidae In," explains how difficult it was for rappers from smaller cities to break through:

The challenge of that is that somebody in New York, they have big opportunities. They're around the stuff. We're not around it, so we're struggling four times as hard as them, for real. We've got to wait till somebody comes to the city or we've got to leave out the city to try to go and find people to get them to listen to our music. We don't have big record companies and all that. We don't have none of that, so we've got to really put a gang of effort to try to make it, go out of state and just grind, grind, grind. People from New York, Miami, the West Coast or whatever, they've got it right there with them. It's not that hard. If I was staying in New York or LA, I probably would have made it because I'd have been grinding so tough that you probably couldn't have helped but seen me.[36]

Rappers Create Their Own Opportunities

Their lack of connections to the music industry did not prevent rappers from the South and Midwest from turning advances in recording technology to their advantage. Previously, few artists were able to use studios because they could not afford to buy and store the equipment necessary to record music. Recording equipment was typically large and heavy and required at least two large rooms in order to operate. But as smaller recording equipment became available and personal computers became capable of recording and storing music, making professional-sounding music outside a studio became possible for a new generation of artists.

These rappers, eager to get their music heard, skipped the steps of recording an album and shopping a demo to a record company. Instead, they simply made their own albums and released them themselves through their own small record companies, which were typically run out of their homes. Sometimes, after creating a name for themselves by selling their albums in the streets and to select record stores, these tiny record companies were able to land a deal with a regional distributor.

The larger distribution ensured that the albums of southern artists were available in more than just their own city. Rap journalist Matt Sonzala explains:

This breakthrough happened because the Southern artists had to work harder to get noticed than artists in New York or Los Angeles. While the artists on the East and West coast are surrounded by media outlets and other industry aids, the artist and labels in the South, long shunned by their Eastern and Western contemporaries, had to get on the road and work their regions on their own. . . . Houston's Rap-A-Lot Records laid the South's foundation with the Geto Boys and became the backbone of the emerging Southern scene in the early and mid-90s.[37]

Many southern rappers created such a presence in their own region that the major labels signed them to recording contracts. Says prominent Mississippi rapper David Banner,

If you look at the South, most of us didn't come from demos or having one hot verse on the mix CD. Me, Lil Jon, T.I., Ludacris—we all put out independent albums. We'd all sold hundreds of thousands of records before we got signed [to major labels]. I had more spins than 85 percent of the people that was in the urban department of Universal before I got signed to Universal. So I think that people should respect us as artists and as businessmen.[38]

Master P Hits the Clubs

One of the best of the rappers and businessmen was Master P. Born in New Orleans, the rapper relocated to Richmond, California, about 20 miles (32km) north of San Francisco, and opened a record store, No Limit Records. Master P paid attention to what kind of rap his customers were buying and in the early 1990s decided to launch his own career as a rapper on his own No Limit Records label. Master P noticed that rap fans still wanted to hear hard-hitting gangster rap, even though the major record companies were moving away from it because of the violence associated with the genre after the deaths of 2Pac and The Notorious B.I.G.

After tirelessly promoting himself and No Limit in the Bay area and such southern states as Louisiana and Texas, Master P and other No Limit artists, including Mystikal and Silkk the Shocker, became a force in independent rap music. Rather than make harsh, mid-tempo music like many gangster rappers before them, they rapped over up-tempo beats that were faster and easier to dance to. Other acts, especially the popular Memphis rap acts 8 Ball & MJG and Three 6 Mafia, also made this style of up-tempo gangster rap and sold millions of albums in the late 1990s.

Eminem Makes a "Shady" Hit

In the mid- and late-1990s, rappers from cities in the South and Midwest became respected national rap stars for the first time. Detroit rapper Eminem was the biggest of these artists. Backed by production from former N.W.A member Dr. Dre, Eminem made controversial antigay statements and recorded a number of songs that seemed to endorse violence, similar to what N.W.A had done nearly a decade before him. In the book Angry Blond, *Eminem reflects on the making of his smash single "The Real Slim Shady":*

I was tellin' the bass player and keyboard player to play something till I liked it. So they kept [messing] around . . . till Tommy (one of Dre's keyboard players) played the first few notes of "The Real Slim Shady" and I jumped up and said, "What was that?" I then asked him to do something different with it. Make it go up, then down. He did a couple of different things with it until I was like "Right there." I then ran and got Dre to come listen to it. They added drums. Now, this all happened on a Friday. We had a meeting on Saturday with the label and they asked, "Well, did you come up with anything?" I played them "The Way I Am" and they said, "It's a great song. It's just not the first song." Originally, they were talkin' about "Criminal" being the single, but I told them to let me take this [beat] ("The Real Slim Shady" instrumental) over the weekend and I'd have the rhyme written by Monday. Then we'd see if it worked. If it didn't, then [forget] it. . . . I came in on Monday, recorded it, and was done.

Detroit rapper Eminem became one of the biggest rappers in the 1990s.

Atlanta Gets Crunk

The progression of gangster rap into music that could be danced to gained the most momentum in Atlanta. Artists in that city developed a type of music called "crunk," a fiery style typified by aggressive production and choruses chanted like cheers at a pep rally or sporting event.

The up-tempo beats of Master P's gangster rap encourages fans to dance.

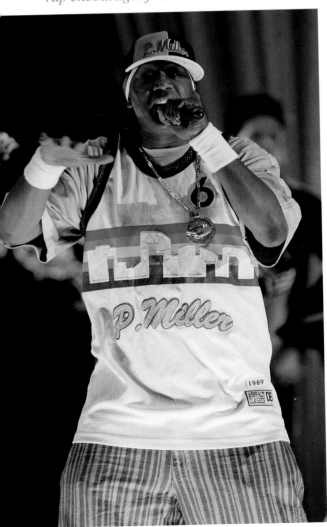

Atlanta-based Lil Jon & the East Side Boyz are the premier crunk artists. The trio emerged in 1996 with its first album, the independently released *Who U With, Get Crunk: Da Album*. In a 2002 interview, Lil Jon explains why Atlanta became so popular for the crunk style of rap:

Atlanta's such a big melting pot. You've got so many different people from so many different areas here. You've got so many different artists that come here just to go to the studio and work. You've got so many big events that happen here. The records that come out of here are exposed to a lot of people that just come in town for the weekend for this or that. That helps to spread the records out. Atlanta artists, we make records straight for the clubs. If your record ain't hitting in the club, then these [people] ain't gonna buy your [music]. You got [artists] that got hot club records that aren't even on the radio that's selling a lot of records in Atlanta. Eventually, those records translate to the radio, but that's the main thing about the Atlanta music scene: We make records for the clubs that will get the clubs cracking. If it ain't getting the clubs cracking, then they ain't buying it. That's how we look at putting the records together.[39]

Crunk Will Last

In this November 2004 interview with the author, Lil Jon explains why he thinks the rap subgenre of crunk is here to stay:

It's funny, now people are coming to me like, "So, how long do you think crunk can last because it's getting commercialized? What is going to happen when crunk gets too commercialized?" I'm like, crunk is the essence of energy. It's hard to commercialize the essence of energy like that. That's why Usher came to the crunk world. The crunk world didn't go to Usher. The same thing with Ciara. They came to our world. We didn't go to their world. We aren't sounding R&B on a track. We're sounding like we sound. They're sounding crunk on the track. It seems like being, southern artists, they always want to down you and dis your music. They treat crunk like early hip-hop, like they were like, "This ain't going to last. It's a fad." No. Crunk is a way people live the lives in the South. This is how we live. People live and die to get crunk. It's a way of life, a culture and people don't understand. They just look at the records and think that that's what it's all about, but it's the way we live in the South.

Crunk artist Lil Jon (center) poses with the East Side Boyz in 2005.

DJs Make a Comeback

Thanks in large part to the success of southern rap acts in the emerging club scene and the increasing presence of rap music on radio stations, DJs again became major hip-hop figures in the mid-1990s. Therefore, even as rap became more and more prominent and graffiti artists and B-boys were increasingly marginalized by mainstream

DJ Kid Capri spins records in 2005. Capri was one of the first DJs to create mixtapes consisting solely of rap songs.

society, DJs were able to develop healthy followings.

To the bigger rap movement, the DJ's main purpose was to support the rapper, if a DJ was used at all. But a number of other developments allowed DJs to become significant fixtures in the rap scene themselves. A crop of DJs who created mixtapes, released their own albums, toured and performed with rock and roll groups, and appeared on television programs became increasingly popular.

Mixtape Culture Explodes

Excitement and energy describe the mixtape culture that has come to be a formidable force in the rap industry. Mixtapes were around long before

"Rapper's Delight" was released. In the early and mid-1970s, DJs assembled the most popular R&B, soul, funk, and disco songs and put them on a cassette tape. These were called mixtapes because the songs from various artists were mixed together. The DJs then sold the tapes at their performances and in the streets to fans, thereby earning money and recognition.

Once rap songs became popular in the early 1980s, DJs included rap songs on their mixtapes. Later in the 1980s, DJs such as Kid Capri and Ron G realized that they could also make mixtapes solely of rap songs and that those mixtapes were even more popular among their customers.

In the 1990s, mixtapes, especially those in New York, began to feature unreleased music from artists. Individual DJs tried to forge relationships with star rappers in the hopes that the rappers would give them a copy of new songs first. This arrangement gave such DJs as Funkmaster Flex and DJ Clue? a reputation for having the newest music and made them celebrities in their own right.

Even though rappers enjoyed the exposure and attention their songs garnered from mixtapes, many DJs earned the ire of record companies because their mixtapes featured music that the companies did not authorize for release. DJs therefore labeled many mixtapes "for promotional use only" and did not technically offer them for sale. That way, the record companies could not sue the DJs because they could claim they were not selling the mixtapes.

DJs Release Major Albums

As DJs regained their status throughout the 1990s, a number of high-profile DJs graduated from releasing their own self-funded and self-distributed mixtapes to signing deals with major record companies to release albums nationally. The albums from DJs came in a variety of formats.

Pioneering mixtape DJ Kid Capri released *The Tape* in the early 1990s. Although the album featured the popular DJ rapping, it failed to garner much interest. It took several years for a mixtape DJ to get another chance to put an album out on a national level. Then popular club and radio DJ Funkmaster

Flex broke through in the mid-1990s with *The Mix Tape* series of albums, which were like traditional mixtapes. The albums contained a number of classic rap songs as well as songs exclusive to the album.

DJ Clue?'s *The Professional* album, which arrived in 1998, was in the format of DJ Clue?'s popular mixtapes. It featured all original material from the hottest rappers and R&B artists of the moment, including DMX and Jay-Z.

Another type of album put out by DJs featured the DJs scratching over their own self-produced beats. Released by such DJs as the X-ecutioners, these albums were showcases for the mixing, scratching, and production skills of the DJ, unlike the majority of mixtapes and the albums put out by DJ Clue? and DJ Kayslay, among others, which featured popular rappers rather than the DJs' own turntable dexterity.

50 Cent Changes the Mixtape Landscape

Mixtapes and mixtape DJs remained a largely New York phenomenon until about 2002, when 50 Cent changed the way mixtapes were made. 50 Cent was released from his recording contract with major label Columbia Records when he was shot and almost killed in 2000. After recovering, 50 Cent resumed making music. Unable to get a new recording contract, 50 Cent took instrumental versions of popular songs and made his own covers of them. He

Rapper 50 Cent, shown here at the 2003 MTV Movie Awards, helped popularize mixtapes nationwide.

then compiled the cuts with his DJ Whoo Kid onto mixtapes and released them to the underground mixtape scene in New York. DJs clamored to feature 50 Cent's material on their mixtapes.

The strategy paid off for 50 Cent, who featured his rhyme crew, the G Unit, on many of his mixtape releases. With his name building in New York and radio stations playing his mixtape songs on the radio, something that had rarely happened before, several record companies started pursuing the rapper. In 2002, 50 Cent signed to Dr. Dre's Aftermath Entertainment and Eminem's Shady Records. After selling more than 10 million copies of his own albums, 50 Cent still releases mixtapes, although less frequently than he did before signing with Dr. Dre and Eminem.

The explosion of the mixtape culture, thanks in large part to the success of 50 Cent, increased the standing of DJs in the hip-hop world. In 2005, DJs such as Green Lantern and DJ Drama released mixtapes (today recorded on CD) that earned as much attention as some albums. In fact, the mixtape DJs are so popular and have such big followings that many rappers give their new songs to mixtape DJs before they give them to anyone else—including their record label.

Rock Groups and Television Embrace DJs

As mixtape culture developed in the late 1990s and more DJs secured major record deals, DJs became more prominent through their work independent of rappers rather than with them. Even though rappers typically distanced themselves from DJs, the DJs got a boost from a seemingly unlikely source: rock groups. Rock acts that incorporated some rapping into their work, such as Limp Bizkit and Kid Rock, featured DJs during their live performances. Around the same time, television shows such as *The Chris Rock Show* and *Chappelle's Show* featured DJs to segue the program into and out of commercial breaks.

After several years in which their value diminished, DJs are again a visible and crucial portion of the hip-hop landscape. With their high visibility, several DJs also have become international draws, a key component of hip-hop's global explosion.

Chapter Seven

Hip-Hop: A Global Force

As hip-hop developed in the mid-1970s, DJs were the cornerstone of the culture. So when DJ and hip-hop pioneer Afrika Bambaataa organized the first European hip-hop tour in 1982, he established himself—and, by default, DJs in general—as the culture's unofficial ambassador around the world. The Bambaataa tour included DJs, B-boys, rappers, and graffiti artists. By introducing Europe to all aspects of hip-hop culture, the tour allowed each segment of the culture to evolve outside the United States.

So, even though rap has been the most recognized and popular component of hip-hop culture since it exploded in the late 1980s, the other components have enjoyed sustained levels of respect and acclaim throughout the world. Also, as in the United States, where each segment of hip-hop culture grew out of other forms of art, international hip-hop followed a similar path by morphing into new styles and sounds based on the American originals and the business models of American hip-hop businessmen.

English Rappers Score

In England, rap quickly developed its own scene. London rapper Derek B released an album in 1988 on Profile Records, also home to Run-D.M.C. Even though he did not become a major rap force in America, he nonetheless helped establish the London rap scene because his album encouraged other aspiring British rappers to record their own material and develop their own style of rap.

Starting in the early 1990s, trip-hop, an English form of hip-hop typified by a mixture of break beats and down-tempo electronic music and popularized by Massive Attack and Tricky, began to catch on in Europe and eventually the rest of the world. The music was especially popular in dance clubs, and its deep, hypnotic grooves were said to be enjoyed more thoroughly if a person was on a drug-induced "trip"—hence the name trip-hop.

A segment of trip-hop soon evolved into garage, a style of English hip-hop with faster and heavier drum patterns. This intense style garnered international acclaim thanks to conversational white rapper The Streets, female rapper and R&B singer Ms. Dynamite, and hard-core rapper Dizzee Rascal. All three artists, each with a distinctive sound, style, and image, enjoyed critical acclaim in such high-profile American music magazines as *Rolling Stone* and *Entertainment Weekly*. In fact, in its January 16, 2004, issue, *Entertainment Weekly* gave Dizzee Rascal's *Boy in da Corner* album the lead review, a

English trip-hop artist Tricky performs in 2003. Trip-hop, an English form of hip-hop, is popular in dance clubs because of its trancelike, hypnotic sound.

distinction reserved for an album of particular interest or merit.

MC Solaar Introduces French Rap

Three years after Derek B brought British rap international attention, French-based rapper MC Solaar earned an international following because of his nimble raps and the jazz-inspired music over which he rapped. His first album, 1991's *Qui Seme le Vent Recolte le Tempo (He Who Sows the Wind Gathers the Tempo)*, was an early example of quality rap performed in a lan-guage other than English. As writer Don Snowden explains in his AMG All Music Guide review of the album:

The debut disc from MC Solaar is a clear signal that quality hip-hop can exist outside the U.S. and the English language barriers. Most of his lyrics read as "I'm the man" MC boasts and shout-outs to the Paris hip-hop crew, but the French rapper has superb flow and a masterful producer in Jimmy Jay, an absolute natural when it comes to creating sonic pastiches/collages

The collaborative efforts of Diddy (left) and Reggaeton rapper Daddy Yankee are showcased during the 2005 Billboard Latin Music Awards

to fit the lyrics. It's French hip-hop and therefore a softer, gentler sound with the music more on the acid jazz tip to match the rhythm and flavor of Solaar's native tongue. . . . Its an impressive debut and important historically—by pairing a rapper and producer in perfect sync with one another, it gave early French hip-hop a sound and tone of its own from the beginning.[40]

Reggaeton Strikes a Chord

As French rap evolved, people in other countries began creating their own styles of rap, too. Reggaeton, from Puerto Rico, is a popular, typically energetic hybrid of rap and reggae, the indigenous music of Jamaica popularized by the laid-back "roots" style of Bob Marley and the more aggressive, rap-influenced dancehall style of Buju Banton, Sean Paul, and others. Hip-hop and reggaeton, which is typically performed in Spanish, share many similarities. Reggaeton is, in the words of popular artist Tego Calderon, "the new way the youth here in [Puerto Rico] express themselves; mainly it was a form of expression among the poor. It started out the same way as hip-hop did. Initially, it was totally underground. In a 10-year span people got used to listening to our music, and the music earned a space in radio shows."[41] Like hip-hop acts, reggaeton artists have a number of different musical styles. Calderon incorporates political messages into his

material, while Daddy Yankee and Pitbull have scored international hits with their infectious dance music.

There are several signs that reggaeton's appeal is increasing. Def Jam Recordings, the rap label made famous by LL Cool J, Public Enemy, and others, announced in July 2005 that it was launching Roc La Familia, a label whose roster will include reggaeton artists. Furthermore, Daddy Yankee appeared on the cover of the July 2005 issue of the American rap magazine the *Source* and Pitbull has worked extensively with accomplished American rap producer Lil Jon. A number of other American rappers are also collaborating with reggaeton artists. New York rapper Noreaga, for one, has started incorporating reggaeton into his own rap music, while Fat Joe and 50 Cent are among the rappers who have collaborated with Calderon.

The national newspaper *USA Today* featured a reggaeton article as the lead story in its Life Section on August 5, 2005. The genre is becoming increasingly popular in the United States, especially in cities with large Hispanic populations. DJ Camilo of New York's hip-hop radio station HOT 97 explains, "What really made it [reggaeton] explode in New York was so much demand in the Latin community. It really started with the mixtapes and the buzz in the streets. I would be working clubs six and seven nights a week and seeing how people kept requesting it. Once I took it to the radio, it opened up so many avenues."[42]

Reggaeton Roots

In an article titled "Spanish-Spiced Hip-Hop" that was published in USA Today, Steve Jones explains the roots of reggaeton, whose evolution in the Caribbean and South America mirrors that of hip-hop in the United States:

Reggaeton has its roots in Panama, where Spanish-language reggae was developed in the 1970s by Jamaicans who were descendants of immigrants who helped build the Panama Canal. The new hybrid eventually found its way to Puerto Rico, where rapper Vico C (Luis Armando Lozado Cruz) produced the first Spanish-language hip-hop record in 1985. Ultimately, the two influences combined into a music that appealed to urban youth in Puerto Rico and eventually evolved into contemporary reggaeton.

Much like hip-hop in the USA, reggaeton was initially dismissed, but continued to grow. Hector el Bambino, reggaeton's equivalent to rap production mastermind Dr. Dre, says that because it was a blend of so many musical styles, it cut across cultural lines and began spreading throughout the Caribbean, Central America, and South America, and then filtered into the USA. The music—which like hip-hop has faced criticism over its sometimes violent and sexually charged lyrics—gave birth to its own entrepreneurs, record labels, and distributors, who flourished independent of corporate assistance.

The Japanese Hip-Hop Scene

As reggaeton gains popularity throughout the world, Japan remains prominent on the world hip-hop scene. As in the 1970s in the Bronx, each segment of hip-hop culture is celebrated there with virtually equal attention. The Japanese affinity for B-boys is so strong that there is a Japanese Rock Steady Crew, as well as a number of other B-boy crews, including ZOO.

Two of Japan's first and most recognized hip-hop artists are DJ Krush and DJ Honda. Best known for his production prowess, DJ Krush specializes in deep, meditative, and moody beats that have hip-hop–inspired percussion and also include traditional Japanese music. DJ Honda, on the other hand, is known for his minimalist, drum-heavy production that sounds similar to that of New York rap producers of the mid-1990s.

Even though many Japanese rappers and fans do not understand or speak English, that has not stopped hip-hop from being accepted and practiced in their country. As writer Geo Hagan notes, "The Hip Hop movement is itself a revolution that started in the streets and has grown to be the most influential cultural force the world over. There are kids in Japan that don't understand a word of English, but can still recite a Jay-Z album from beginning to end."[43]

Jay-Z Helps Punjabi MC

In addition to having millions of fans in the United States and Japan, Jay-Z helped catapult Punjabi MC to stardom in 2003 when he appeared on the remix to Punjabi MC's "Beware of the Boys." The word *Punjabi* refers to a member of the majority people of Punjab in northwestern India, and Punjabi MC, who lives in England, took his stage name as a nod to his Indian heritage.

Jay-Z's appearance on the song made it a hit in the United States, but more importantly, "Beware of the Boys" introduced a hip-hop take on bhangra, a Punjabi dance music traditionally performed during harvest festivals and weddings, characterized by the beating of a large two-headed drum. The song, as well as the work of American producer Timbaland and others, helped popularize bhangra with

DJ Krush, one of Japan's first hip-hop artists, includes traditional Japanese music in some of his songs.

rap fans around the world. In his review of *Beware*, the album on which "Beware of the Boys" appears, writer Dan LeRoy explains the album's international significance: "As an authentic antidote to hip-hop's superficial Indian infatuation, *Beware* is most welcome; what it augurs for future musical meetings between East and West makes it most important as well."[44]

Worldwide Struggle

Fans around the world hold American rappers such as Jay-Z in high regard, but they often feel a special connection with rappers from their own countries, who rap in the native language about topics relevant to their homeland. Rappers around the world have taken their American predecessors' cue by using their raps to discuss political issues and express their outrage at social injustices. In Mexico, for example, rappers discuss drugs, violence, and Mexican Indian pride, while in Brazil rappers discuss life in the nation's ghettos, known as favelas. In the African country of Ghana, rappers discuss how AIDS is ravaging the country, while in Israel rappers offer their opinions regarding the Israeli-Palestinian conflict.

While the work of these rappers resonates most strongly with people in their own countries, it has increasingly been gaining notice in other parts of the world. The *Source*, the most recognized American rap magazine, has Latino and French editions that discuss matters of political significance, and also features an annual international section in its domestic edition that highlights the work of hip-hop practitioners around the world. Also, thanks in part to the Internet, which allows songs to be transferred electronically, it is as easy for a rap fan in Turkey to listen to a protest song by an Israeli rapper as it is for a Kenyan enthusiast to hear the work of a Brazilian rap artist famous for writing political songs.

China Controls Rap

Even though rap retains its rebellious edge throughout much of the world, in China many rappers create music the government endorses and even promotes. In an article titled "You Can't Get a Bad Rap Here," *Los Angeles Times* staff writer Ralph Frammolino explains that Chinese rappers release tame music that embraces government policy:

Instead of often obscene and violent tales from the inner city, . . . leading rappers here are taking to the stage with lyrics that glorify national pride, celebrate tourist attractions and preach against the dangers of adolescent impulsiveness. One group is so proud of its songs that it has affixed a sticker to its debut album asking fans to share it with their parents. State controlled television features public service announcements in rap about caring for the environment and respecting elders, leading one academic to suggest that hip-hop

Fugees Find International Audience

The Fugees, a rap trio, emerged in the mid-1990s and became one of the world's most popular rap groups thanks to its musical brand of thoughtful hip-hop. The following is a portion of writer John Bush's biography of the group from the AMG All Music Guide:

The trio formed in the late '80s in the New Jersey area, where Lauryn Hill and Prakazrel Michel ("Pras") attended a local high school and began working together. Michel's cousin Wyclef Jean ("Clef") joined the group (then called the Tranzlator Crew), and the trio signed to Ruffhouse/Columbia in 1993. [The group eventually renamed] themselves the Fugees (a term of derision, short for refugees, which was usually used to describe Haitian immigrants). Though the group's debut album, *Blunted on Reality*, was quite solid, it reflected a prevailing gangsta stance that may have been forced by the record label. No matter how pigeonholed the Fugees may have sounded on their debut, the group had obviously asserted

their control by the time of their second album, *The Score*. With just as much intelligence as their jazz-rap forebears, the trio also worked with surprisingly straight-ahead R&B on the soulful "Killing Me Softly with His Song," sung by Lauryn Hill. Elsewhere, Clef and Pras sampled doo wop and covered Bob Marley's "No Woman No Cry," giving the record familiarity for the commercial mainstream, but keeping it real with insightful commentary on their urban surroundings.

The Fugees gained popularity by infusing soul into their hip-hop albums.

has become the unofficial music of the Communist government.[45]

In fact, Frammolino notes that the writings of former Chinese ruler Mao Zedong inspired a Chinese rap album that was released in 2003 in conjunction with his 110th birthday.

But not all Chinese hip-hop supporters find the Chinese government's in-

Missy Elliott displays a signature shoe manufactured by Adidas. Rap celebrities are popular spokespeople for consumer products.

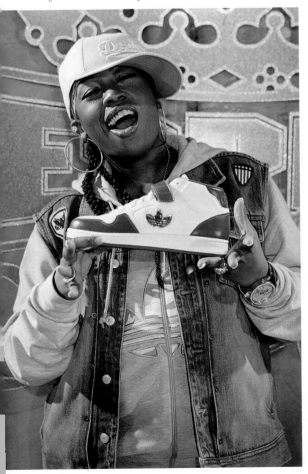

volvement with the work of rap artists appealing. As Beijing-area disc jockey Chen "MC Allan" Shen explains, Chinese rappers "can't curse, they basically have to say life is great, life is beautiful, nothing's wrong. . . . It's not hip-hop.[46]

Hip-Hop as Global Business

What hip-hop is and is not continues to be defined as it spreads throughout the world. The globalization of business and the increased ease of international travel have helped each element of hip-hop culture become a significant tool for selling products internationally for a variety of corporations. Today, rap albums are among the best-selling albums around the world. Furthermore, rappers are now viewed as reputable spokespeople and are paid to promote such products as soft drinks and deodorant in advertising campaigns used by major corporations in the United States and Europe.

A prime example of hip-hop's international commercial viability is the presence rappers have in the tennis shoe market. Shoe companies, which realized the importance of embracing hip-hop in the 1980s with Run-D.M.C. and in the 1990s with Master P, fully incorporated hip-hop culture in the new millennium. By the end of 2003, Jay-Z had his own "The S. Carter" shoe through Reebok, 50 Cent had his own "The G Unit" shoe through Reebok, and Nelly teamed with Nike to release a limited-edition "Air Derrty" shoe. These deals, promoted around the world, marked the first time

Jay-Z, Master of All Trades

In January 2005, Jay-Z took over as president and CEO of Roc-A-Fella Records and Def Jam Recordings. In July 2005, Jay-Z announced the launch of Roc La Familia, a Def Jam subsidiary that would release albums from reggae, reggaeton, calypso, tribal, and West Indian artists. Writer Jason Birchmeier details the first portion of Jay-Z's music career in the AMG All Music Guide:

Jay-Z reigned over the New York rap scene throughout the late '90s and early 2000s and steadily built up the Roc-A-Fella Records dynasty in the process. The Brooklyn rapper made his splash debut in 1996 and cranked out album after album and hit after hit throughout the decade and into the next. Jay-Z became so successful that Roc-A-Fella, the record label he began with Damon Dash, became a marketable brand itself, spawning a lucrative clothing line (Roca Wear); a deep roster of talented rappers (Beanie Sigel, Cam'ron, M.O.P.) and producers (Just Blaze, Kanye West); a number of arena-packing cross-country tours; and even big-budget Hollywood films (*Paid in Full, State Property*). While such

success is amazing, Jay-Z's musical achievements outweigh the commercial achievements of his franchise. Every one of his albums sold millions, and his endless parade of singles made him omnipresent on urban radio and video. Moreover, he retained a strongly devoted fan base—not only the suburban MTV crowd but also the street-level crowd as well—and challenged whatever rivals attempted to oust him from atop the rap industry.

Entrepreneur and rap artist Jay-Z makes a television appearance in 2005.

that nonathletes were used to endorse athletic shoes.

As rap's influence continues to grow, the other segments of hip-hop culture have grown too. Graffiti, for instance, regained its commercial acceptance in the 1990s and has again become a bankable practice. Journalist Laura Checkoway explains, "By 2000, art galleries, once shunned by those who conceived of graffiti as public art, were selling canvases with five-figure price tags, and high-end designers hit the runways with graf-inspired creations."[47]

Hip-Hop as International Bridge

In addition to being a prime source of commerce throughout the world, hip-hop has also been used as an international unification tool. For instance, in 2002, a rap song was promoted to celebrate the end of the Muslim holiday Ramadan. As writer Anwar Iqbal explains,

This year the end of Ramadan in New York will be celebrated with a hip-hop song called "Muslim." An African-American group called Native Deen will perform this and other songs in front of an expected audience of 1,000 on Dec. 7, when Muslims around the world celebrate the end of the fasting month. The Washington-based group borrows its name from an Arabic word "deen," meaning faith, and fuses African-American and Islamic cultures to convey its message: pray five times a day, do not smoke or drink and be proud of Islam. After its New York concert, the group plans to visit Britain Dec. 13–17 on a five-city tour."[48]

A Hip-Hop World

Hip-hop, which started out as something fun to do in Bronx neighborhoods in the 1970s, has become a billion-dollar business that reaches into virtually every aspect of life. Indeed, thirty years after its inception, hip-hop's influence is almost everywhere. Rap songs are among the most popular on the urban and pop radio stations. Major motion pictures regularly feature rappers in starring roles. International turntable organizations thrive in the United States, Germany, and Japan. Many streets in metropolitan areas around the world have some sort of street art, whether it is illegal graffiti, a commissioned mural, or a painting completed with a hip-hop flair.

As it continues to evolve, hip-hop shows little sign of losing its hold on popular culture around the world. Andre Harrell, founder of Uptown Records, who helped launch the careers of Diddy, Mary J. Blige, Jodeci, Heavy D & the Boyz, and others, recognizes the universal appeal of hip-hop culture. "Rich, poor, Asian, Hispanic, black, white, they're all part of the hip hop generation," Harrell says. "Hip hop just gives everyone an opportunity. Everybody knows where it comes from, everybody loves it. And it's never going away"[49]

• Notes •

Chapter One:
The Roots of Hip-Hop Culture

1. Quoted in Greg Kot, "Bambaataa: 'All Music Is Dance Music,'" *Chicago Tribune*, October 12, 2004. www.chicagotribune.com.
2. Universal Zulu Nation, The Music World of Afrika Bambaataa. www.zulunation.com/afrika.html.
3. Quoted in Kot, "Bambaataa."
4. Quoted in Billy Jam, "Creator of the Scratch: Grand Wizard Theodore," Hip Hop Slam, 2001. www.hiphopslam.com/articles/int_grand wizardtheo.html.

Chapter Two:
Hip-Hop Gains Momentum

5. Quoted in Jenny Eliscu, "The Music Q&A," *Rolling Stone*, September 4, 2003, p. 62.
6. Jayo Felony, in-person interview with author, Glendale, California, April 26, 2005.
7. Quoted in Kot, "Bambaataa."
8. QD3, in-person interview with author, Studio City, California, March 23, 2005.
9. Kot, "Bambaataa."
10. The Reverend Run with Curtis L. Taylor, *It's Like That*. New York: St. Martin's, 2000, p. 30.

Chapter Three:
The Golden Era of Rap

11. Quoted in Austin Scaggs, "The Music Q&A," *Rolling Stone*, August 7, 2003, p. 30.
12. Stephen Thomas Erlewine, "Salt 'N Pepa," AMG All Music Guide. www.allmusic.com.
13. MC Lyte, in-person interview with author, Chicago, Illinois, February 6, 2003.
14. Fabolous, phone interview with author, February 2003.
15. Quoted in Reginald C. Dennis, liner notes, *The Very Best of Big Daddy Kane*. Warner Bros. Records and Rhino Entertainment, 2001.
16. Big Daddy Kane, phone interview with author, March 2003.
17. Stephen Thomas Erlewine, "Public Enemy," AMG All Music Guide. www.allmusic.com.

Chapter Four: Gangster Rap

18. Schoolly D, phone interview with author, March 2003.
19. David Mills, "Los Angeles' Gangsters of Rap, Escalating the Attitude," *Washington Post*, May 20, 1990.
20. David Mills, "Rap's Hostile Fringe," *Washington Post*, September 12, 1990.

21. J.D. Considine, "Rap Capital Shifts from N.Y. to L.A.," *Baltimore Sun*, April 23, 1989.
22. Quoted in John Leland and Linda Buckley, "Number One with a Bullet," *Newsweek*, July 1, 1991.
23. Mills, "Los Angeles' Gangsters of Rap."
24. Richard Harrington, "Rap's Unheard Riot Warning," *Washington Post*, May 27, 1992.
25. LL Cool J with Karen Hunter, *I Make My Own Rules*. New York: St. Martin's, 1997, p. 190.
26. Mills, "Los Angeles' Gangsters of Rap."
27. Lorraine Ali, "The 90s Era—Smells Like Teen Spirit," *Rolling Stone*, May 15, 1997, p. 97.
28. Quoted in Laura Parker, "Rap Group Acquitted in Florida," *Washington Post*, October 21, 1990.
29. Jonathan Yardley, "Art and the Oeuvre of 2 Live Crew," *Washington Post*, October 22, 1990.

Chapter Five:
The Rap Business Explodes
30. Julio G, phone interview with author, March 15, 2005.
31. Phyllis Pollack, phone interview with author, March 14, 2005.
32. Tomica Wright, phone interview with author, March 15, 2005.
33. Layzie Bone, phone interview with author, March 9, 2005.
34. Young Noble, interview with author, March 18, 2005.

Chapter Six: The Rise of the South and of the DJ
35. Quoted in Lang Whitaker, "Double Shots," *XXL*, August 2003, p. 86.
36. Chingy, in-person interview with author, Los Angeles, California, October 27, 2004.
37. Matt Sonzala, "Rise of the South," *The Official Guide to the Source Awards*, 2003, p. 72.
38. Quoted in Hillary Crosley, "Blessed by Lil Scrappy, Produced by Lil Jon, David Banner Gets Certified," MTV.com, May 6, 2005. www.mtv.com/news/articles/1501362/20050506/story.jhtml.
39. Lil Jon, phone interview with author, August 2002.

Chapter Seven:
Hip-Hop: A Global Force
40. Don Snowden, "Qui Seme le Vent Recolte le Tempo," AMG All Music Guide. www.allmusic.com.
41. Quoted in Marcano M. Ninoska "Q and A with Tego Calderon," *Baltimore Sun*, November 11, 2004.
42. Quoted in Steve Jones, "Spanish-Spiced Hip-Hop," *USA Today*, August 5, 2005.
43. Geo Hagan, "The Pimping of an Icon," *Rime* 8, 2003, p. 18.
44. Dan LeRoy, "Beware," AMG All Music Guide. www.allmusic.com.
45. Ralph Frammolino, "You Can't Get a Bad Rap Here," *Los Angeles Times*, November 12, 2004. www.latimes.com.

46. Quoted in Frammolino, "You Can't Get a Bad Rap Here."
47. Laura Checkoway, "State of the Elements," *Vibe*, September 2003, p. 114.
48. Anwar Iqbal, "Americans Add Hip-Hop to Ramadan," United Press International, November 27, 2002. www.upi.com/view. cfm?StoryID=20021127025310-5260r.
49. Quoted in Emil Wilbekin, "Art Imitates Life," *Vibe*, September 2003, p. 150.

• For Further Reading •

Books

Chuck D with Yusuf Jah, *Fight the Power: Rap, Race, and Reality.* New York: Delacorte, 1997. Commentary from the Public Enemy leader about rap, race, and America.

Jasmine Guy, *Afeni Shakur: Evolution of a Revolutionary.* New York: Atria, 2004. A biography of the mother of rap star 2Pac.

Tamara Palmer, *Country Friend: Soul Adventures in Dirty South Hip-Hop.* San Francisco: Backbeat, 2005. A look at the vibrant southern rap scene.

Tricia Rose, *Black Noise.* Hanover, NH: Wesleyan University Press, 1994. A scholarly look at rap music and hip-hop culture.

The RZA, *The Wu-Tang Manual.* New York: Riverhead Freestyle, 2005. A look into the world and culture of the Wu-Tang Clan, an acclaimed New York rap group whose members include Method Man and the RZA.

Adam Sexton, ed., *Rap on Rap.* New York: Delta, 1995. A collection of articles and essays that examine the positive and negative aspects of rap.

Tupac Amaru Shakur, *The Rose That Grew from Concrete.* New York: MTV Books/Pocket Books, 1999. A book of poetry from the rap star.

Web Sites

AllHipHop.com (www.allhiphop.com). A thorough Web site that includes news, features, reviews, and often reliable rumors about what is going on in the rap world and in hip-hop culture.

The Original Hip-Hop Lyrics Archive (www.ohhla.com). A Web site with extensive lists of lyrics from hundreds of rappers.

• Works Consulted •

Books

Martha Cooper, *Hip Hop Files: Photographs: 1979–1984*. Cologne, Germany: From Here to There, 2004. An invaluable look at hip-hop's formative years through photos and interviews with a number of the culture's early practitioners and documentarians.

Eminem, *Angry Blond*. New York: ReganBooks, 2000. The Detroit rapper explains the story behind the making of many of the songs on his first two major-label albums.

Jacob Hoye and Karolyn Ali, eds., *Tupac: Resurrection 1971–1996*. New York: Atria, 2003. A look at the life of the rapper through his own words, his letters to friends, and photos.

LL Cool J with Karen Hunter, *I Make My Own Rules*. New York: St. Martin's, 1997. A biography about the personal life of rap's most enduring artist.

The Reverend Run with Curtis L. Taylor, *It's Like That*. New York: St. Martin's, 2000. A biography from one-third of Run-D.M.C.

Randall Sullivan, *Labyrinth*. New York: Atlantic Monthly, 2002. A detective investigates the murders of 2Pac and Notorious B.I.G.

Liner Notes

Reginald C. Dennis, *The Very Best of Big Daddy Kane*. Warner Bros. Records and Rhino Entertainment, 2001.

Periodicals

Lorraine Ali, "The 90s Era—Smells Like Teen Spirit," *Rolling Stone*, May 15, 1997.

Ray Benzino and Dave Mays, "What's Really Hood?" *The Source*, October 2003.

David Browne, "The Cat in da Hat," *Entertainment Weekly*, January 16, 2004.

Laura Checkoway, "State of the Elements," *Vibe*, September 2003.

Jenny Eliscu, "The Music Q&A," *Rolling Stone*, September 4, 2003.

Entertainment Weekly, "Monitor—Honors," October 24, 2003.

Geo Hagan, "The Pimping of an Icon," *Rime* 8, 2003.

Austin Scaggs, "The Music Q&A," *Rolling Stone*, August 7, 2003.

Lisa Schwarzbaum, "Ask the Critic: Gift Rappers," *Entertainment Weekly*, October 17, 2003.

Matt Sonzala, "Rise of the South," *The Official Guide to The Source Awards*, 2003.

The Source, "Planet Rock," May 2003.

Lang Whitaker, "Double Shots," *XXL*, August 2003.

Emil Wilbekin, "Art Imitates Life," *Vibe*, September 2003.

Internet Sources

@149st, "History Part 1 (Draft)." www.at149st.com/hpart1.html.

Jason Birchmeier, "Bone Thugs-n-harmony," AMG All Music Guide. www.allmusic.com.

———, "Jay-Z," AMG All Music Guide. www.allmusic.com.

John Bush, "The Fugees," AMG All Music Guide. www.allmusic.com.

Hillary Crosley, "Blessed by Lil Scrappy, Produced by Lil Jon, David Banner Gets Certified," MTV.com, May 6, 2005. www.mtv.com/news/articles/1501362/20050506/story.jhtml.

Stephen Thomas Erlewine, "Beastie Boys," AMG All Music Guide. www.allmusic.com.

———, "Public Enemy," AMG All Music Guide. www.allmusic.com.

———, "Salt 'N Pepa," AMG All Music Guide. www.allmusic.com.

Billy Jam, "Creator of the Scratch: Grand Wizard Theodore," Hip Hop Slam, 2001. www.hiphopslam.com/articles/int_grandwizardtheo.html.

Greg Kot, "Bambaataa: 'All Music Is Dance Music,'" *Chicago Tribune*, October 12, 2004. www.chicagotribune.com.

Steve Kurutz, "Kool DJ Herc," AMG All Music Guide. www.allmusic.com.

Alexs Pate, "Poets with Attitude," *Washington Post*, 1992. www.washingtonpost.com.

Universal Zulu Nation, The Music World of Afrika Bambaataa. www.zulunation.com/afrika.html.

• Index •

• Picture Credits •

• About the Author •

Soren Baker has had more than 1,900 articles published, the overwhelming majority of them focusing on hip-hop culture. The Maryland native writes for a host of publications, including the *Los Angeles Times, Scratch, Down,* and *Rime.* His work has also appeared in the *New York Times* and the *Chicago Tribune,* among others. Baker wrote and produced VH1's Ultimate Albums episode on Eminem's *The Marshall Mathers LP,* and he also wrote and produced Chingy's *Powerballin'* DVD and Tech N9ne's *The Tech N9ne Experience* DVD. He and his wife live in the Los Angeles area.